ROBERT MULLER

Most of All,
They Taught Me Happiness

Foreword by Norman Cousins

Robert Muller

AMARE MEDIA LLC
Los Angeles, California
2005

Published by AMARE MEDIA LLC
P.O. Box 35360
Los Angeles, CA 90035-0360

First published in 1978 by Doubleday & Company Inc.

Cover photograph © madphoto.com
A grateful acknowledgment to Gail Brendle for design consulting

Library of Congress Catalog Card Number 78-52110

ISBN 1-932943-05-6

Amare Media First Printing August 2005

Printed in the United States of America

For Barbara Gaughen-Muller, my wife,
a wonderful model of happiness,
and to all our children and grandchildren
who represent the possibility of a happy world
of peace and love
for all human brothers and sisters

Publisher's Note

This text was originally published in 1978 and some of its expressions may occasionally appear outdated... please overlook the form, in light of the timeliness of the ideas expressed within.

Contents

Preface to the New Edition

At the age of 82, I am very moved and excited that *Most of All They Taught Me Happiness* is being republished. I am rejuvenated and feel enthusiastic about sharing again the precious lessons I learned from magnificent human beings of all walks of life.

It is my greatest wish that these stories will inspire readers to be aware of all their blessings and to work for the happiness of others. All of us can decide to apply our talents, passion and energy to cultivating the welfare of all living beings.

We can embrace our differences and our common aspirations, cherishing and tending to our common natural habitat. At this crucial moment in history, it is our responsibility to support one another until our precious Planet flourishes as the miraculous Paradise that God always meant it to be.

Robert Muller
June 2005

Foreword

At a time when it is intellectually fashionable to declare that the entire metabolism of history has gone berserk, it is heartening to meet a man who not only is completely free of nihilism but who also can articulate the compelling reasons for believing that the cause of civilization is not beyond human intelligence.

Everyone who has any interest in, or access to, the inner workings of the United Nations sooner or later comes across Robert Muller. His current title may be the longest on the Secretariat's roster. He is director and deputy to the Under-Secretary General for Inter-Agency Affairs and Co ordination.[1] In his thirty years of service with the UN, which began with the writing of a winning essay on world government in a contest sponsored by a French Students' Association for the UN, he has held a variety of positions: He worked in the Financial Branch of the UN Department of Economic Affairs, became secretary of the UN Capital Fund Committee, helped Paul Hoffman — former administrator of the Marshall Plan — to establish the UN Development Program. He served as special assistant to the Under-Secretary General for Economic and Social Affairs, as chief of the Steel and Engineering Unit of the Economic Commission for Europe, as political adviser to the UN troops in Cyprus, as counselor to the Secretary General of the UN Trade and Development Conference, as associate director of the UN's Natural Resources Division, and as director of the Budget Division — before assuming the responsibility of co-ordinating the work of the thirty specialized agencies and programs con-

[1]Written in 1978. Subsequently, Robert Muller rose to the position of Assistant-Secretary-General

cerned with humanitarian, economic, social, scientific, cultural, and environmental problems.

I first met Robert Muller a decade ago, through Secretary General U Thant, and quickly recognized Robert Muller as a magnificent anomaly. He obviously did not fit the ultracool or tough school of diplomacy — nor did his conversation bear any resemblance to the somber talk often heard in the corridors of the United Nations. In a place where the ways of nations readily breed cynicism and distrust, Robert Muller was immediately recognizable as a dedicated and confident internationalist — open intellectually and spiritually to any ideas connected to the making of a better world.

Born in Belgium and raised in Alsace-Lorraine, Robert Muller was subjected to the Nazi occupation of World War II, joined the French Resistance under an assumed name, was captured, and was imprisoned. He holds a doctorate in law and economics from the University of Strasbourg and degrees in Economics from Heidelberg and Columbia universities. He is married to Margarita Gallo, a former UN diplomat and delegate from Chile.

Implicit in Robert Muller's "recipes for happiness" (an earlier title for this book) is a belief I share — the belief that pessimism and optimism are significantly more than opposite moods. Just as despair sets the stage for its own omens, so reasoned hope provides the essential nutriments for a flowering of the spirit that enhances life, thereby contributing regenerative energies to the shared living environment. The fact is that we do not know enough to be pessimists. Throughout history, man's supposed limitations have given way before the power of the human imagination, the ability of the human intellect to conceive of and do what has never been done before. The vision of life as it ought to be acts as a powerful magnet in the advance of the human race. Pessimism operates in a narrowed field of vision that fails to take into account the possibilities at the outer edges of experience.

Two events in 1945 had a profound effect on thoughtful people concerned with human purpose: the birth of the United Nations, an organization dedicated to saving succeeding generations from the "scourge of war," and the dropping of the first atomic bomb.

Mankind had simultaneously drafted a blueprint for a rational future and designed the means of obliterating life wholesale. Confronted with this coeval conjunction of promise and peril, many believers in man's perfectibility consciously chose, as did Robert Muller, to dedicate themselves to working for the long-range ideal of a world community organized under law and justice. The choice was, by definition, that of an optimist.

But even an optimist has need of a philosophy to propel him through times of discouragement and uncertainty. Certainly, the years since Robert Muller first joined the United Nations in 1948 have been sufficiently full of discouragement and uncertainty to test his philosophy. Into the past three decades have been compressed more impending crises, more brushes with madness, more change, more thrust, more tossing about of men's souls, than has been previously spaced out over most of the human chronicle. Nuclear stockpiles have continued to grow and proliferate as we ride precariously astride an accelerating technology. The danger so well described by Alfred North Whitehead — that events might outrun man and leave him a panting and helpless anachronism — has become more than a figure of speech. We live on a combustible planet, with our destiny threatened from all directions — by our increasing numbers, by the ravishing of nonrenewable resources, by the poisoning of the environment that sustains us, by intractable human institutions. For those who underestimate the human potential, it is a dour and gloomy picture. But the optimist knows that it is our view of ourselves and our connection with the universe that can make the difference.

What doomsayers overlook are those very things that define a human being: the capacity to envision life as it could be, to think in new dimensions, and to be aware of new possibilities. Pessimism and cynicism stem from a sense of hopelessness and helplessness, and human beings have never been helpless. The transient failures that have pockmarked history reflect periods of philosophical poverty. But given a transcendent vision, people have proved themselves capable of uniting across their differences to continue the steady human advance, particularly when it is clear that their destinies are interlocked.

Herein, as Robert Muller and other optimists-by-choice know, lies the realizable potential of human beings and human institutions such as the United Nations; for in the world of humans, the ultimate division takes place within societies, not among them. The division is between those who value life and rejoice in the beauty and wonder of the universe, and in the things that set us apart as a species — and those who hold life to be cheap.

The recurring question is: How do we revitalize and gain acceptance for the idea that life is the highest value? We have viewed the human habitat from outer space and noted that the universe itself does not hold life to be cheap. Life may or may not be a rare occurrence among the billions of galaxies and solar systems that occupy space. In our particular solar system, however, we are reasonably certain that life occurs on only one planet. Of all the magnificent forms of life on planet Earth, only one — the human species — possesses certain faculties that in combination give it supreme advantage over all the others. And among those faculties is a creative intelligence that enables man to reflect, anticipate, and speculate, to encompass past experience and visualize future needs — and to make rational choices. And there are endless wondrous faculties — of hope, conscience, appreciation of beauty, kinship, love, faith — that have yet to be fully understood.

We are increasingly concerned with how self-understanding can be used in the cause of human welfare — to create a peaceful human community, united by common values and inherent kinships rather than divided by differences that are accidents of geography and quirks of history. Among the encouraging developments of the past quarter century is a new literacy from the crossfertilization of ideas and cultures made possible by the speed of communications and travel.

Whatever the uncertainties of the future may be, of these facts we can be sure: The oncoming generations will have to operate in a world arena; be at home in many lands, among many peoples; comprehend many philosophies and psychologies; and be open to approaches as yet uncharted. They will need to have special knowledge, certainly; but they will need something far more important: an intense awareness of the conditions under which the values essential to the future of mankind can be created and maintained. They will need living examples of the conspiracy of love that Teilhard de Chardin has said will be essential to man's salvation. Robert Muller is involved in such a conspiracy.

Philosophical excursions invariably come full circle to the conclusions promulgated by sages throughout recorded history — the conclusions that man cannot safely ignore the life force at the center of his being (by whatever name it is called), that the dignity of man has its inception in the individual, that man's security lies not in transforming nature but in transforming himself, and that it is impossible to talk about the necessary transformation without using the word "love." What Robert Muller has done in sharing his encounters with events, people, places, ideas — in tendering his "recipes for happiness" — is to give us operational definitions of love. The frustrations that make us unhappy arise from an inability to make life-affirming connections between ourselves and others, between ourselves and the circulatory systems within the universe that sustain us.

Our frustrations also arise from the mistaken belief that the complexities of life preclude happiness — that life is something from which we must flee to be happy. Robert Muller rejects any such notion on the premise that it is an unaffordable indulgence in futility from which we should spare ourselves and others. He has developed what Cyril Connolly spoke of as a "conscious affinity with Nature [that] forms the shield of Perseus through which man can afront [sic] the Gorgon of his fate." He meets and drinks to life on its own terms — exultantly, reverentially. He believes in the natural goodness of his fellow human beings and in the effectiveness and infectiveness of undeviating optimism. For him, as for Whitehead, "the present is holy ground" out of which the future proceeds. Robert Muller justifies the gift of life in his daily encounters with himself, with others, with his universe. He sanctifies life by savoring it. He reverences life by opening himself to it, by interpreting its vibrations positively, by drawing from it all the benign influences that can be made to flow in human interactions.

Having lived at the center of events in a period of unique human evolution, he has attempted to share with others the formulas that let him remain happy and hopeful in the face of somber and complex problems. His formulas derive from a perspective essential to happiness: He does not feel trapped by time and space; he knows himself to be a positive element in an orderly, evolving universe. He has asked himself, "What is the objective and meaning of life?" His answer: "To be happy, to feel fully the miracle of life, and to be endlessly grateful for it."

He has deliberately chosen to impart his garnered wisdom informally, anecdotally, without somber preachment or ostentation. He would like to see others join with him to build a "rich literature of recipes for happiness" — to dispel the gloom; to give us faith in ourselves, in mankind, in the meaning of our adventure in the universe.

This brings us back to the question of how to gain acceptance for the idea that life is the highest value. Perhaps it is best gained by being introduced to people like Robert Muller, who refuse to be intimidated by the complexities and loose ends of the present, knowing that complexities are the natural habitat of incapacitating cynicism. Perhaps we should arrange for more encounters with people who have discovered that "happiness is not external to man," that it is "a genial force within him" that wants liberating — with people who are aware of life's preciousness and its fragility, people who develop to the fullest the potentialities and sensitivities that come with life, people who apply their intelligence to the cultivation of conditions congenial to fruitful life, who cherish the human habitat, who use their free will to make life-giving, life-sustaining, life-enhancing, life-affirming choices.

Perhaps we should encourage more people to talk about sacredness without overwhelming its meaning with religiosity.

Among the things I have learned is the importance of stepping back now and then to view the world from the perspective of an astronomer or an archaeologist — to relocate oneself in time, in place, in the flow of evolution. In the centrifuge of the twentieth century, we tend to become disoriented, and values take on a free-floating quality. This disconnection gives rise to irreverence — not the irreverence that peels back the layers of sham, but the irreverence that is directed against life itself.

Civilization gets its basic energy not from its resources, but from its hopes. The tragedy of life is not death, but what we let die inside us while we live. We need not fear the consequences of opening our homes, our hearts, or even our nations. It is a privilege to be able to introduce an open man, one who opens himself fully to his readers in the pages that follow.

Norman Cousins
1978

VOLUME ONE

Lessons from the War

Thank You, Dr. Coué

Every morning before rising, and every evening on getting into bed, shut your eyes and repeat several times this little phrase: "Every day, in every way, I am getting better and better." It might save your life.

When I studied at the University of Heidelberg during the war, I lodged in a boardinghouse located in the Hauptstrasse near the Karlstor. Students from several occupied countries resided there, together with Germans who were allowed to study because they had been wounded or because they were needed as doctors or technicians in Hitler's army.

In a room next to mine, on the top floor of the building, lived a Yugoslav named Slavko Bosnjakovich. He was a tall, soft-spoken, aristocratic young man, endowed with the finest features. Despite his youth — he was twenty-seven years old — he had been a colonel in the Yugoslav army. Released from German prison camp, he had come to Heidelberg to study law. His intelligent face carried a dreamy and superior quality, intermingled with considerable strength drawn from his hawklike nose. His complexion was very pale, almost transparent, and his light gray eyes gave him at times a rather distant appearance. We were great friends and became very fond of each other. We were both dreamers and full of expectations about life. I liked his distinguished calm outlook and intelligence, and he my animal-like passion for life and my carefree, wild behavior and laughter. We spent innumerable hours together, either in his room or in mine, discussing life, death, and the future of the world. To this day, I can recall the fragrance of his long, blond Serbian cigarettes, which he smoked from the edge of his lips as if they were a rare, prohibited delicacy.

During the winter of 1942, I wanted to invite him to our home in Lorraine for Christmas, but I knew that my parents, who were living in a rather secluded fashion, would not endorse my invitation. So I abandoned the idea and went home alone. When I returned to Heidelberg in early January our landlady greeted me with sad news: "Your poor friend is severely ill. A few days ago I found him lying on the floor of his room, unconscious, with blood spilling from his mouth. I called a doctor, and an ambulance took him to the hospital. They fear the worst for him. Apparently he is suffering from a very advanced case of tuberculosis."

I rushed to the hospital, where I found my dear friend lying propped up in bed, leaning against a pile of white cushions. He was thinner and paler than ever. The skin of his face was moist, sickly, yellow like wax. His long, thin hands were lifeless and almost transparent. He was breathing softly and carefully, as if not to unduly tax his poor lungs. But in the midst of this image of desolation, his eyes were glowing with happiness when he saw me. His attitude of calm superiority had not abandoned him. He tried to reassure me about his condition, while in my mind I could not help visualizing the ravages that reigned in his narrow, concave chest.

I was allowed to stay with him for an hour or so. When I took leave, he asked me for a favor:

"Could you please go to the university library and borrow for me any books you can find written by a certain Dr. Coué or by his disciples? Bring them to me as soon as possible."

I went there the following morning and found indeed a book by Dr. Émile Coué entitled *Self-mastery Through Conscious Auto-suggestion*,[1] as well as a book written about him by one of his disciples. I thus learned that a doctor from my neighboring town of Nancy in Lorraine had gained worldwide fame for his healing methods based on the confidence and imagination of the patient. In the 1920s he attracted enormous audiences in England and in the United States, where he produced many miraculous cures with his psychological

---

[1]Published under this title in England by George Allen and Unwin, London, and in the United States by Samuel Weiser, New York, under the title *Suggestion and Autosuggestion* by Dr. Émile Coué and C. H. Brooks.

method. His disciple, whose name I have forgotten, had broadened Dr. Coué's views into a philosophy, in which self-confidence, good health, and happiness were the cornerstones of life. I absorbed the contents of the two books in a few hours before bringing them to my friend. To this day I have not forgotten their theme:

Every morning before rising, and every evening on getting into bed, shut your eyes and repeat several times: "Every day, in every way, I am getting better and better." One can add one's own words, and I got accustomed to saying: I feel wonderful, I feel happier than yesterday, I have never felt so good, it is marvelous to be alive and so healthy, etc.

The remainder of the two books were merely elaborations of this central theme. I thought at first that it was a little easy to seek happiness by just repeating to oneself that one felt happy! There was no depth in such a philosophy. But after reflection I agreed that man had indeed the choice of seeing everything in light or in dark and that it was not unwise to start the day with the conviction that one felt good, healthy, and happy to be alive. The amount and intensity of happiness, one's zest for life, one's attitude toward the surrounding world are perhaps determined after all by a basic "internal" decision taken at the beginning of the day.

I brought the books to my friend who, to the great surprise of the doctors, recovered within a few weeks and was released from the hospital.

I have never forgotten Slavko Bosnjakovich and Dr. Coué's method. True enough, as with prayers, I have not always repeated the suggested daily words, but I have instinctively followed Dr. Coué's philosophy of optimism and self-reliance all my life. Many times at the United Nations, when bad news tends to drag me down, I revert to an innermost part of myself, switch on optimism and confidence, and immediately I return to a positive, creative mood. This mysterious quantum change between a negative and a positive current in the total functioning of the human being is the great lesson I have learned from Dr. Coué and Slavko Bosnjakovich. It is a mystery to me. I do not understand it. But it has done miracles for me and it certainly saved my life on at least one if not on several occasions during the war, as the following story will illustrate.

After a series of adventures and an arrest by the Gestapo, I was finally able to cross the border between Germany and France in the summer of 1943. I was working under the false identity of Louis Parizot in a French telecommunications center located in Vichy. In that center, radio messages were recorded that provided the French Government with intelligence information and political news from the rest of the world. It was an ideal situation to infiltrate with members of the Resistance. Several draft evaders from Alsace-Lorraine had found refuge and a job in it. I got an administrative position that enabled me to warn my friends in the technical center, located in the woods outside the city, of impending inspections by the Germans. Their visits had to receive the prior consent of the French authorities, and I was able to obtain complete information.

I had been working there for a few months when one evening, in my hotel room, I noticed that someone had gone through my possessions. It was almost imperceptible, but I had the feeling that there was something wrong, and I asked the hotelkeeper if anyone had entered my room. "Yes, two workers from the electrical company checked it." I could not know whether it had been a routine inspection by the French police, or if the Germans were on my trail, or if electrical workers had indeed displaced some of my belongings.

The following morning I was sitting in my office when I received a telephone call from the guard at the entrance of the building. Like most French governmental services in Vichy, ours was located in a former hotel, in this case the Hotel de Grignan. The guard told me that three gentlemen wanted to see me on behalf of a friend named Andre Royer. I asked him to have them wait for a while and then let them come to my office on the second floor. My heart had jumped violently when I heard the name of Andre Royer, for the news had just reached me that this good school-friend of mine from my hometown in Lorraine had been arrested by the Germans during a raid on the University of Strasbourg and evacuated to the city of Clermont-Ferrand. The men who were on their way to my office were possibly

Germans. I told my secretary to receive them, to find out what they wanted, and to let me know by telephoning the secretary of a colleague in a nearby office where I took refuge.

After a while the telephone rang and I heard my secretary say to the other girl:

"I am looking for Mr. Parizot. Do you know where he is? Three gentlemen from the police want to see him."

This message was clear enough. When the phone hung up, I heard loud shouting. A man with a heavy German accent was screaming at my secretary:

"*Si fou ne me tites pas ou est Parizot the fou fais fousiller.*" (If you do not tell me where Parizot is, I will have you shot.)

To gain time for thought, I decided to proceed to the hotel's attics, and I asked the secretary who had harbored me to give a message to one of my colleagues who was a member of the Resistance. He joined me soon thereafter and gave me the following report:

"You have little chance of escape, if any. There are five or six Gestapos in the building. They are systematically searching offices and appear quite relaxed, for they know that you are here. The entrance to the hotel is blocked and a prison van is stationed at the curb. To hide here in the attics or climb on the roof will not help. You know perfectly well that they will shoot you down like a pigeon."

He left me after these cheerful words, promising to return if there were any new developments, and I found myself alone to consider the trap I was in:

"This is the moment of all moments," I thought to myself, "to keep cool and in full command of my mental and physical capabilities." I suddenly remembered Dr. Coué. "I must feel relaxed and even elated about this situation." Following the good doctor's advice, I repeated to myself that it was indeed an extraordinary and thrilling adventure for a twenty-year-old youth to be trapped in a hotel, pursued by the Nazis. Would it not be exciting if I could play a trick on them and slip through their fingers?

Having thus switched my perspective to a positive, confident frame of mind, I felt relaxed, even happy and cheerful, without any fear or thought of failure whatever.

I began to think calmly and decisively. My sequence of thoughts was as follows: "Nothing is hopeless in this world. There must be at least one chance in a thousand to escape from this situation. I must find it, and for that, I must concentrate on the mentality of the Nazis. They know that I am in this building. They are several. They have guarded the entrance. They are convinced that they will get me and that it is only a matter of time and *Gründlichkeit* (thoroughness). There is no classical means of escape. I must think of something that would be foreign to their psychology."

I let my thoughts wander in this direction and examined various options, of which all but one led to certain arrest and possible death. A little flicker of hope arose in the following suggestion:

"There are many people in the hotel. My best chance of escape is to become part of the crowd. Why not walk downstairs and go straight to the group of people who must be gathered on my floor? The Nazis certainly do not expect me to do that. The worst that could happen would be to be arrested. But this is likely to happen anyway. If I have any chance at all, it is by doing the one thing the Germans do not expect me to do: to walk straight to them."

I put my plan immediately into action. I changed my physical appearance as best as I could, wetting my hair with water from a faucet in one of the former maids' rooms, and parting it on the side. I took off my glasses and lit a cigarette to gain a relaxed posture. Once on the fourth floor I seized a file from a desk and placed it under my arm. On the third floor I caught a glimpse of two Germans who were inspecting offices, but there was no disquietude. It seemed that few people knew what was going on. But it was a different story when I walked down the majestic staircase from the third to the second floor.

A large gathering of people had assembled, mostly officials who had been asked to vacate their offices. I could not see very well without my glasses, but nevertheless I was able to distinguish a group dominated by shiny spots: These must be the bald heads of the Germans, I surmised, and I decided to walk straight up to them. An infinitesimal fraction of silence set in when my French colleagues saw me appear on the staircase, but they immediately understood what I was trying to do, and they chatted louder than before in order to cre-atc a diversion. I walked up to the group of Germans and recognized my secretary, whom they were still interrogating. I asked her calmly:

"What is all this turmoil about?"

She answered very composedly:

"These gentlemen are looking for Mr. Parizot." I expressed surprise:

"Parizot? But I just saw him a few minutes ago on the fourth floor!"

"*Schnell hinauf!*" (Quickly upstairs!) shouted one of the Germans, and the whole group moved into action and ran upstairs!

I maneuvered casually for a few more minutes, in case I was being observed by one of the smarter Nazis. My French colleagues were careful not to pay any attention to me, and they returned to their desks. I went to the office of a compatriot, Dieffenbacher, from my hometown, and asked him how I could get out of the building.

"The main entrance is guarded, but there may be a way of getting to the garage through the cellars. The French superintendent downstairs should be able to help you."

I walked down to the entrance lobby and talked to the *concierge*. There was indeed an exit through the cellars, and he led me to it. Midway he suddenly took fright, thinking of the possible reprisals by the Germans. I persuaded him to help me and, under his guidance, I finally reached the garage, which was full of bicycles. I took a good, sturdy one and rode to the house of a former French officer who was a member of the underground. There I waited for a few days until the search had abated and then proceeded to St. Etienne in the Auvergne, where I joined an active *maquis* (underground resistance group) in the hills.

I learned later that the Germans had been so thorough and convinced of finding me that they had even unrolled old carpets stored in the attics!

After the war, I met again with my secretary, Madeleine Grange, who told me that when I walked down the staircase, she was reciting to herself:

"*Passera, passera pas, passera, etc. . . .*" (Will pass, will not pass, will pass, etc. . . .)

I also learned from her that the Gestapo had a picture of me, a detail that I fortunately did not know, for if I had, it is possible that even Dr. Coué's method would not have helped me.

Ever since, and after several other instances when Dr. Coué's method saved me from very difficult situations during the war, no one has ever been able to convince me that optimism is not preferable to pessimism. Truly, my optimism has often been challenged and resented as being contrary to the prevailing rules of life, but I have never been given a solid reason to join the other side. The complexity of world affairs demands that those who deal with them be confident and strive to do their utmost even in the face of greatest difficulties. The sad chorus of pessimists only makes matters worse. To be a human is to live on the positive and sunny side of life that God has given us. Optimism, hard work, and faith are not only in our highest self-interest, they are also the affirmations of life itself. To give up, to see only hurdles and dead ends ahead is not the right attitude toward the great privilege of life. I was fortunate that one of my compatriots from the wartorn borderland of Alsace-Lorraine taught me this at an early age. It is perhaps in regions that have suffered the most that people acquire extra reasons to hope and an iron will to cope with the obstacles presented in life.

Thank you, Dr. Coué, thank you from the bottom of my heart.

How to Read the Newspapers

Read the newspapers from a distance, with a great dose of distrust, and do not let them poison your life.

Incessant bad news is one of the main causes of the world's unhappiness. In my long international career, I have known several attempts to correct this situation with information systems aimed at emphasizing "good," "positive," "peaceful," and "optimistic" news instead of bad, negative, aggressive, and depressing news. All these plans have failed so far. As a matter of fact, the greatest attempt ever to establish a proper information service for mankind namely, United Nations Information — encounters great difficulties. Indeed, if there has ever been a vast effort to provide peoples with factual information about the state of the world, it has been made by the United Nations and its specialized agencies. There is not a subject on earth that has not been brought to the world organization for study, diagnosis, discussion, recommendation, and international action. Placed side by side, the dozens of yearly statistical surveys produced by the United Nations and its specialized agencies constitute an unmatched and truly extraordinary encyclopedia of knowledge about our planet and its people. And in the huge sum of information issued by the UN system there is a considerable amount of good news. Not a single day passes when I do not find some record of progress and reason for hope in the United Nations documents that reach my desk.

But I very seldom see this positive news reported in the media, which seem to be doing an admirable job hiding the UN from the people. Press releases, radio services, television coverage, and documentary materials are widely distributed by the UN to the news

media. But are they really used? It does not seem so. Many UN corre-
spondents lament that positive developments are usually rejected by
their home editors. They claim that the public wants bad news, exciting news. As a result, people learn infinitely more about what is
wrong in the world than about what is going well. What then is the
solution? To hope for the media to improve is rather wishful thinking. It remains therefore basically a question between the individual
and massive institutions that spread unhappiness. It is a situation in
which the individual is powerless. As in all similar cases, be it captiv-
ity, sickness, dictatorship, poverty, working for a bureaucracy or for a
huge corporation, there is only one escape: reliance upon the internal
strength of the individual, his resilience, his resistance, his own outlook on life, his secret liberty that no one on earth can take away from
him. It is simply a matter of self-protection against an unwanted
environment. And it is an easy case to win, for no one is forced to read
the newspapers, to listen to the radio, or to watch television.

The person who taught me this simple lesson was my mother. In
our hometown in Lorraine we were fortunate not to have any morning newspaper. The *Courrier de la Sarre* was delivered at midday, but
my mother read it only in the evening after supper, when all her day's
work was finished. She had a very strange way of reading it. Sitting at
the kitchen table under the adjustable lamp hanging from the ceiling,
she read it with an acute air of suspicion written all over her face. She
perused it from a distance, as if it were poisonous. Her lips were dis-
dainful and drooping with disbelief. It took her usually only a few
minutes to go through the entire paper, reading only the headlines,
the birth, marriage, and death announcements as well as the daily
installment of a novel. Then she pushed it aside and stored it to light
the oven. I asked her once why she acted like that and she answered me:

"Son, as long as I have lived, be it in peace or in wartime, under
French or German rule, in prosperity or in depression, I have noticed
that there is always the same amount of bad news in the papers. It
seems to be some kind of basic human law. Therefore, I do not want
to be influenced by it. I have my own house and family to care for.
That is all I can do. I read the paper only to be informed of catastro-
phes that might come too close to us, such as another war. Otherwise

I could not care less. The world will never be happy and at rest. It will never rain to the satisfaction of everyone. So why should I make my life miserable by reading bad news?"

I have followed her example all my life and seldom read any newspapers. I merely have a quick look at the index to see if something really world-shaking has happened. During more than twenty years of commuting between my little village in the Hudson Valley and Manhattan, nobody has ever seen me read a newspaper. As a result, I am immune to New York's and to the world's daily neuroses, and hence an infinitely happier person. During the first few years, when I was a young man, it was more difficult to protect myself from that environment. So I read, every morning on the train, writings of some of the great masters of literature and philosophy, to brace myself against the mental beating that awaited me in the gigantic city. Again, in the evening, my old masters lifted me to higher spirits and helped me to face my family as a good-humored, normal human being. I will never forget the astonishment of one of my American neighbors when I showed him a book I was reading assiduously on the train: Bossuet's *Sermon on Death!* This remarkable text helped me put my daily work into proper perspective and was my best armor against the hammerings and neurotic spasms of city and world news.

Today I no longer need books, for I have found my own philosophy and inner happiness amid the jungle. Like the ducks swimming on the Hudson, I have grown impermeable feathers that protect me from the daily news pollution. Like my father, I do not listen to the radio and seldom watch television, and like my mother, I read the newspapers cursorily, condescendingly, from a distance, and with an infinite dose of suspicion. Thanks to the wise example of my parents, I am as particular about the nutrition of my mind as I am with the nourishment of my body. I seek the food, news, images, words, and sounds that I consider good for myself   that is, that bring me health, happiness, and self-fulfillment — and I carefully avoid toxic materials that others wish to impose on me.

Perhaps someday the news media will change and bring happiness and hope to the people. Until then, I will be quite content to descend into my tomb without having read the appalling newspapers of this planet.

Happy Even in Prison

A human being is always a prisoner of something. The only real freedom is within ourselves.

One of the severest tests a person can undergo is imprisonment. I will not enter into the circumstances that led to my arrest by the Nazis during the war when I tried to cross the border. Of relevance to the subject of happiness is my experience in one of the prisons I visited on that occasion and that brought me straight back to Dr. Coué.

The jail was located in the cellars of an apartment building that the Gestapo used as their headquarters in the city of Metz in Lorraine. Today, as I write these lines, it occurs to me that the prisoners were kept there only for a few days until their interrogation was over. But at the time we did not know this, and I remember that nothing was more painful for us than uncertainty about our fate. The Nazis had selected the apartment building for its large number of cellars — about twenty — separated by solid concrete walls, which were part of the foundations of the edifice. They were elongated, parallel storage rooms for the tenants, equipped with small ventilation windows opening onto the street or an internal courtyard. The windows were located just under the ceiling, a little above the height of an average person. Each of the cells contained two wooden bedframes and was meant for two prisoners. Four to six people could live in one for a short while, sleeping on the floor. But at times, I counted up to thirty men standing erect next to each other, packed like passengers in a Tokyo or New York subway car during rush hours. When we were only a few, we talked about trivial subjects, as we feared that a German agent might be hidden among us. When we were many, we remained silent in order to save oxygen, which was our major preoccupation. Thirty pairs of lungs breathing air in such a small area created quite a problem. The odor in the cell was nauseating. The toilet facilities consisted of a pail kept in a corner. We watched with concern its contents grow. Every morning we were allowed to take a walk in the courtyard where we washed our faces and emptied the pail in an outhouse. But above all, this short time was used to fill our lungs with the most precious good on earth: fresh, crystal-clear, delightful air! Until then I had had no idea how wonderful fresh air could taste! During the rest of the day, there was nothing to do, except to watch one's respiration and listen to the footsteps of a guard locking up other prisoners or fetching one for interrogation. The hours were long, heavy, full of silent human despair. No one talked or moved, prostrated as we were by the shortage of air. By evening, a good number of prisoners had usually been transferred to other jails and we could sleep on the floor, but for fear of asphyxiation we often preferred to slumber in an upright position.

The best place in the cell was under the window, where some fresh air was gently gliding down the slanted finishing of the concrete wall. I let the others struggle for it and chose instead to stay near the door, where a small peephole let a tiny rivulet of air seep in. I kept my nose close to it and inhaled as much as possible of the precious element. My mind was actively figuring out what I could do. To escape was out of the question. Furthermore, we had arranged our crossing of the border in such a way that we could not be accused by the Nazis of having tried to evade the German army. I had planned the escape with a student whose parents lived in Metz, and we were arrested together. We still had to agree on a few details to co-ordinate our answers during interrogation. Our cells were apart, but prisoners in the cellars that separated us conveyed from one to the other the few cryptic messages needed to consolidate our case. After that, there was nothing left to do, and I wondered how I could react against this nightmare. I remembered Dr. Coué's good advice: Be the happiest man of earth, wherever you are and whatever you do. Seen from that point of view and with a good dose of imagination, the fact of being in prison became a rather interesting experience. Under normal peacetime conditions, I could have never expected to have such an adventure. This was a unique occasion to observe the reactions, feelings, and thoughts engendered by imprisonment. Moreover, I had to dominate the situation instead of being dominated by it and test whether Dr. Coué was right. What I needed most was a "positive" activity. After scrutinizing various possibilities, one occurred to me. When our guard came from upstairs with another prisoner, I told the guard that I badly needed fresh underwear and begged him to let me go near my suitcase, which was kept with the belongings of the prisoners in a separate cellar. The cellmates had told me that he was a poor fellow who was quite ready to render such a service provided I gave him some of my belongings. I therefore winked at him when I made my suggestion. He acquiesced and took me to the storage room, where I found my small suitcase. I gave him as much of its contents as possible: soap, shirts, a sweater, keeping for myself a chunk of smoked ham, an undershirt, a brief, and, above all, a pencil. Back in the cell, I began to write a novel on the door, starting in the upper left corner and writing minutely, not knowing how long I would be kept in that place. To escape mentally from the wretched cell, I imagined a ravishing girl, fell madly in love with her, and wrote the story of our idyll. I dreamed about beautiful snow-covered mountains high up under clear, sunny skies. I described rivulets of cold, pure water trickling its way through melting snow under the gentle warmth of a glorious spring. I filled a valley with edelweiss and gentians. I built a cabin worthy of a shepherd or a poet. I have not lived much in the mountains, but it was in that dark, putrid cellar that I discovered their real beauty and meaning: the sense of liberty, the feeling of purity, the closeness to God and to the infinite, silent universe. To this day I can remember the cracks and irregularities of the door, its colonial green, and how difficult it was to keep my pencil sharp, scraping it against the rough concrete wall.

Thus, during those somber and miserable days, once again, through will and imagination, I was able to keep in good mental shape and even to attain a certain degree of happiness. I noticed that most prisoners resorted to some similar method in order to escape from prison. Their minds were "outside," with their families, their friends, their jobs, their gardens, or their hobbies. Later in life, when

I sojourned in India, I learned that Tibetan monks often ask to be locked up in rock cells where they train themselves to escape immaterially, to join the stars and the universe, and to regain their physical body and prison at will. Our efforts were more modest but basically not different.

We were interrogated several times over a period of days and then transferred to another prison, the former seminary for priests of the Archdiocese of Metz, an old, stern building with large, austere rooms. My friend and I shared the same cell. Two beds and benches constituted the furniture, and we had a good view over the gardens through large barred windows. Each morning we went through the classical prison routine: Take our blankets, shake them in the courtyard, and walk around in circles with other prisoners.

We were left in total ignorance of our fate. This was the hardest part of imprisonment. We would have received with relief the news that we had been condemned to six months or a year of jail, but we wanted to know, we needed to visualize a date of freedom. Then one morning, as we were speculating once more about the future, a German guard entered our room and told us that we were free to go.

We said good-bye to each other. My friend rushed home and I went to the railroad station where, while waiting for the departure of the next train to my hometown, I had one of the most intense pleasures of my life: to order, to see, to caress, to hold, and to gulp down with heavenly delight an enormous glass of ice-cold, freshly drawn Alsatian beer seeping through its beautiful egg-white collar of bittersweet foam. This was the apex of life. This was the symbol of liberty. From then on, freedom on earth had for me a specific taste: the taste of beer. I was therefore not surprised a few years later, when my father died, that his last gesture before closing his eyes was to bring a glass of beer trembling to his lips. The liquid spilled and the glass broke with his last breath, but he took with him in death the taste of the ultimate drops of freedom. He too had been a prisoner of the Nazis under different circumstances, and when he was freed he rushed to the nearest bar to order a beer! The origin of our strange craving can probably be found in an ancient rite of the Germanic tribes for whom beer was a symbol of liberty.

As I write these lines thirty years later, I have in front of me a tiny piece of wood torn off from one of the bedframes of the Gestapo cell in Metz. On it I had written:

"21 Aout 1943. Gestapo, Metz, soif, chaud, couche par terre, pas d'air." (August 21, 1943. Gestapo, Metz, thirst, heat, lying on the floor, no air.) I had given it to my mother when I got home. She had kept it and, after the war, when I left France to work for the United Nations, she handed it to me with these words:

"Son, always remember what you and your father went through during the war. Never forget your origins and try to be a good man."

What thoughts that little piece of wood still evokes in me today!

Life later confirmed in every respect the correctness of Dr. Coué's advice. My attitude toward the loss of liberty was applicable to a much broader set of human conditions, for, as I advanced in life, I learned that man on his little planet is always, in one way or another, a prisoner of something: He is a prisoner of his time, his beliefs, his class, his possessions, his education, his God, his institutions, his employer, his nation, his culture. He is a prisoner of the biosphere and of the immensely complex life processes that traverse him and link him with the earth. Thus, a few minutes without oxygen will kill him.

Man is jailed in a minuscule solar system lost in a forlorn corner of the universe. And man in all these cells is condemned to death. He knows it, but ignores the time and the way. Yes, man is a prisoner in every direction, except one: within himself. His only freedom is to feel free in his prisons, for man is at the same time a marvelous creation, a tremendous, complex cosmos of his own, a miraculous assemblage about which scientists will still wonder for ages to come. Thirty trillion cells, thousands of miles of vessels, hundreds of automated processes and biological clocks, a marvelously complex and highly developed brain, instantaneous nervous reactions, a phenomenal capacity to learn, to store, to invent, to imagine, to love, and to probe, that is the mountain contained in our living envelope, that is the human person. His brain and heart are able to embrace the entire universe, the moon, the stars, the thoughts, the feelings, the beauty, the ugliness, and the richness of the whole world, past, present, and future. Man is the freest of all beings, liberated by his mind, which knows neither distance nor time. In his cell he can dream of mountaintops and glowing glaciers; deprived of all possessions, he can embrace the totality of life; oppressed or tortured, remain master over his heart and mind; ignored and forgotten, feel like a king on earth. Man in his prison has always a pencil to record his dreams of liberty. He rules over an immense empire during his short stay on earth. To be unhappy, to be ungrateful, not to feel wonder and appreciation for the incredible gift of life is indeed a most foolish and shortsighted attitude. The toughest prison of all is that which man imposes upon himself.

Yes, there is always a way out and plenty of liberty within reach: in an office, in the home, in a garden, in a train, in a plane, in a church, in a crowd, in a monastery, in a prison. In turmoil as in calm, in war as in peace, in talk as in silence, in town as in country, in factory as in nature, man carries with him everywhere a shell of liberty and dreams. And when Dame Death at last catches up with him, he can gently look at her, see brilliant beauty instead of a skull, and bravely say:

"There is always an escape, I believe in immortality, in resurrection, in reincarnation, in death as a joy, as a liberation, as a rejuvenation. Please take my hand and lead me gently to the eternal grounds of peace and beauty, to God, to Brahma, to the universal soul that encompasses all things in heaven and on earth. To vanish into nothingness is impossible. Death does not exist. There must be another life. The contrary would be even more impossible."

I cannot prove it? All right. You prove the opposite.

Man always wins if he wants to. Brandishing liberty, happiness, and joy, he is a king unto death. He is the affirmation of life and of the universe. Each atom of his body was forged in a star. Each atom of his body will return to a star. Everything flows and changes, but nothing can be lost in the universe. . . .

Dr. Coué's method of conscious auto-suggestion had rendered me again a signal service. Together with prayer, faith, detachment from earth, merging with God and the cosmos, it was my only means to

resist. It reminded me of the testimony of a religious leader, Abdul
Bahá, who spent many years in prison and who said:

> I was in prison forty years — one year alone would have been
> impossible to bear — nobody survived that imprisonment
> more than a year! But, thank God, during all those forty
> years I was supremely happy! Every day, on waking, it was
> like hearing good tidings, and every night infinite joy was
> mine. Spirituality was my comfort, and turning to God was
> my greatest joy. If this had not been so, do you think it pos-
> sible that I could have lived through those forty years in
> prison? [Abdul Bahá, "Of Joy and Pain"]

The same applies to all our prisons on earth.

Nightguard at Givors

Have a dream and believe in it. Strong dreams always come true.

August 1944. The night had been calm. Dawn was rising as I stood guard outside the little town of Givors in the valley of the Rhone, near Lyon. There was no longer any great danger of being attacked by the Germans. They were fleeing through the Rhone Valley, pursued by French and American troops. Our assignment was to harass them in their retreat. In the predawn silence of the night, images came back to me of similar watches in the hills of Auvergne, when everyone was asleep in the little hamlet of La Chapelle. The Germans always attacked the *maquis* at daybreak after having approached the hills silently during the night. When the first silver lights of a new day appeared on the horizon, one's ears and eyes were strained to the breaking point. Hidden in the cold, wet bushes, surrounded by a beautiful and peaceful nature, amid the birds' symphony of resurrection, one's sole duty and preoccupation was to discern any sound that would herald a surprise attack and to discharge one's rifle to alert one's comrades.

The war was now coming to an end. The Germans had retreated from Lyon. Our last combat engagement with them was a few days old. Soon I would quit the *maquis*, return to Alsace-Lorraine, see my parents again, and resume my studies.

My thoughts were wandering in the past and in the future. I had always loved people, the world, and all manifestations of the miracle of life. As a child I could watch for hours the clouds run across the moon, possessed by an impossible dream: to be at the top of the world and to understand the laws and mysteries that held everything together. But alas, I knew that this was pure fantasy, and I had pursued my pedestrian studies in my little town with its people and their little problems.

My war adventures and ordeals were now coming to an end. Here I stood, thinking of the future in a world at peace, soon to be freed of Hitler and his hordes.

Suddenly my thoughts rushed back violently to an incident that had just occurred. A few days ago, we had captured a group of twenty young Germans, members of the *Arbeitsdienst*, a paramilitary organization invented by Hitler in order to train young men prior to the enlistment age. During the last months of the war they were given weapons and thrown into combat like regular troops. They feared the *maquis*, for their officers had told them that we did not take prisoners but would shoot them down. Nevertheless, they had surrendered to my appeals in German over a loudspeaker and had trusted my denial of their officers' accusation. I had talked to them and explained that we were not killers but just young men who wanted to get rid of Nazi occupation. Soon they would be free to return to their families and country. Until then, we would keep them prisoners in Givors, where our new headquarters was located. When the attack on Lyon began, I left during the night with members of my group and returned to Givors the following evening. On my return I heard this gruesome story:

The young Germans had all been lined up in front of the cemetery wall and had been shot by a firing squad of our *maquis*. The priest of the town had apparently thrown himself in front of the guns in order to prevent the killing, but he was pushed aside. All twenty young men were dead. I could not believe what I heard and ran to our commander in an indescribable state of furor. Despite my lower rank I shouted at him:

"What is this insane story I hear? I had talked to these young men. They had surrendered against our promise that they would be unharmed. They were almost children. They looked like me, we spoke the same language, they had a mother like you and me, and they had their dreams as we have ours. What madness went into you? What right did you have to take the lives of these boys?"

Commandant Marey answered calmly:

"I must explain to you what happened. Some peasants reported to me that a few days ago, just before our arrival, a big wooden barrack was seen going up in flames a few kilometers from the town. They asked me to go and have a look. I went and I saw one of the most horrible scenes of earth: Dozens of charred bodies were spread among the debris of the burned barrack; some of them had their hands and feet tied with barbed wire; others had nails hammered into their jawbones. There had been a report that the Germans had evacuated some of their political prisoners from Fort Monluc in Lyon to an unknown destination. This was the place. They had thrown cans of gasoline over the prisoners and burned them alive with the barrack. I returned immediately to Givors, assembled your young Nazis in front of the cemetery, told them what their compatriots had done, and had them shot. From their looks it did not seem that they were particularly perturbed. They were arrogant to the very end, almost happy to be sacrificed for their insane Führer and fatherland. . . ."

The faces of these young men came back to my mind. Yesterday they had been alive. Now they were dead for all eternity. Their dreams, their hopes, their hearts, the love of their mothers, the pride of their fathers, all these were gone forever, annihilated by a handful of bullets. Not even a tombstone would bear their names; no notice of their death would be sent to their families, who would wait for them in vain. The image came back to me of my father, who had worn two uniforms and known two wars; of my grandfather, who had had five nationalities and known three wars; and of my cousins, who were now fighting in different uniforms on opposite sides in the present war. The whole world seemed a madhouse. Suddenly an immense determination overpowered me. I looked at the fading moon and stars, my hand clenched my rifle in an iron grip, and I swore to God that I would spend my life working for peace in this wretched world. How I would do it, I had no idea. But I knew that it would be my obsession for the rest of my life. I swore it to the twenty young men whose bodies lay fresh on the ground a few hundred yards from me....

February 3, 1970. Twenty-five years later. I was able to fulfill my dream and have now worked for the United Nations for over twenty years. I did whatever a man could do for peace in this divided and power-drunk world. The United Nations celebrates its twenty-fifth anniversary. I have reflected a lot about humanity's accomplishments and failures during this period. One could cry at the lost opportunities to build a peaceful, more just, and safer world. Most governments have played a selfish game and closed their eyes to the deeper currents of change that have seized our planet. The first atomic bomb exploded six months after the drafting of the UN Charter. The Cold War shattered many dreams of the founders. Trouble spots and conflicts erupted all along a line reaching from Germany to Korea, through the Middle East, Cyprus, and Southeast Asia, diverting the energies and vision of the leaders away from the deeper problems of our time. The world was divided into armed camps. Dozens of airborne hydrogen bombs were constantly circling our globe, and hundreds of nuclear missiles were lurking in the ground and in the seas. Injustice and poverty in the Southern Hemisphere were a blemish for our generation. The historic page of independence had not been completely turned, encountering major resistances in the South of Africa. Governments had given insufficient support to their only decent creation: the United Nations. Bogged down in their daily affairs and games of interests, they were heading blindly and unprepared toward a future they did not even try to understand. Worries and new global problems were inundating the world, generated like colonies of bacteria by the greed, the filth, and the misbehavior of the human race.

And nevertheless, looking at the total balance sheet, I had to recognize that immense progress had also been achieved during this Promethean time: A Third World War had been avoided amid circumstances that could have triggered several global conflicts. Two billion people had been introduced into the modern age.

Colonial empires had crumbled and a billion people had achieved independence. Longevity had increased substantially all over the world, in rich and in poor countries. Most major epidemics had been eradicated, and infant mortality had decreased dramatically. Man had set foot on the moon, and instruments linked by constant communications to our planet were being sent farther and farther into our solar system. More than a thousand satellites and space objects were circling the earth, studying its resources, climate, and environment. We had seen the birth of jet transportation and the bloom of world travel. Man had reached with his tools the abyss of the seas. We had witnessed the harnessing of atomic energy, the birth of electronics, of cybernetics, of laser technology, and the unlocking of many mysteries of matter. Microbiology had opened up exhilarating vistas of scientific advance. Agronomists had become prodigious genetic engineers. Man had extended immensely the horizon of his eyes with giant telescopes, spectroscopes, microscopes, and radars; increased the power of his hands with incredible machines and factories; multiplied the capacity of his brain with computers and automation; and expanded the faculties of his hearing with sonars, radio, and space communications. His knowledge was reaching farther and farther into the universe, deeper and deeper into the infinitely small, farther and farther into the past, ever more distantly into the future. His view of the world was beginning to be total, global, interdependent. Never before had there been such a concern for the fate of the entire human race and for its planetary home. Humankind was standing on the threshold of an entirely new era of evolution.

Yes, what a Copernican experience we had lived since World War II! What prodigious changes had taken place on our globe! I had had the privilege of observing them from the greatest observatory on earth: the United Nations. And it was not individual men or nations who could be credited with the advances; it was humanity as a whole.

But how many times, returning home in the evening, I felt discouraged and frustrated at the slowness of political understanding and international co-operation. Why did governments hesitate so much to put together their hearts, forces, and intelligence to solve humanity's problems? One persistent thought, however, came back stubbornly to me: It could have been infinitely worse. It was indeed a miracle that humans were not slaughtering each other on a worldwide scale and that they had crossed most of this phenomenal period without a new holocaust. If year after year we could continue to avoid a major conflict, perhaps someday we would reap the results and see flourish a new era, an epoch of political maturity endowed with a Copernican vision of all basic relations on earth. The real needs and limits, rights and obligations, present and future, of the human race would then become clear. Political men would finally understand that we lived in an entirely new epoch, which required the co-operation and amity of all and the support and strengthening of the planet's first global institutions.

These thoughts occupied my mind as I was walking on this beautiful February morning from my home to the little railroad station of Ardsley-on-Hudson. Fat gray squirrels were chasing each other from tree to tree. Large black crows were resting on the telephone poles, like vultures in the Orient. Little birds were flitting about, repairing old nests and hunting for food. Schoolchildren were waiting for their yellow buses. Here the world was at peace and busy, while on the other side of the planet humans were killing each other. I took my usual eight thirty-five train to Manhattan where, as every morning, I walked up Forty-second Street to the East River. There, in the tall UN building, I entered an elevator, pressed a button, and reached the thirty-eighth floor. I entered a new office.

It was the happiest day in my life: U Thant, the Secretary General of the UN, had appointed me director in his executive office. I was to be one of his closest collaborators. This time I would meet full-face the challenge of my pledge during the night at Givors. I would be as close as any human being could ever become to the problems of peace and war. But I was prepared for it by many years of experience, thought, learning, and unfaltering love for the human race. I was prepared by all — friends, superiors, and colleagues — who had instilled in me their knowledge, faith, skill, and determination. I was ready to fight without compromise for whatever was good and against whatever was bad for mankind.

As I took possession of my new office, images of certain people entered my thoughts: those of my father, my grandfather, my cousins, and the twenty young Germans of Givors. I took out of my briefcase the photograph of an emaciated young man, dressed in an incomplete khaki uniform, wearing a revolver at his belt. It was one of my few mementos from the war. It could have been one of the young Germans. But it was not. It was my own picture taken while in the underground. I placed it on my desk to remind me every day why I was here and what my dream had been.

My heart was smiling: Dreams, after all, were still possible in our seemingly hard, materialistic world. The advice of the poet, "Be truthful to the dream of thy youth," had lost nothing of its veracity. Man, the little cosmos, was far from being crushed by the modern world. He had a liberty, a range of thought, imagination, and action, a knowledge, and a well-being unmatched by any king or emperor in all human history.

It was the twenty-fifth anniversary of the United Nations. It was the twenty-fifth year without a world war. I was filled with joy at the thought of the innumerable little bricks I could contribute to the edifice of peace in my new position. My dream of the night at Givors had come true. Strong dreams always come true.

VOLUME TWO
Lessons from Adulthood

Two Turning Points

Man's own mind and heart are his greatest friends and treasures.

Reading is certainly one of the great pleasures and enrichments of life. Nevertheless, I have also often felt that excessive reading may be at the expense of personal thinking and imagination. The ideas and dreams of others do not necessarily arouse our own creativity and mental fulfillment: They can stifle them. In principle, there is nothing in a book that cannot be conceived by our own mind and heart. Scientists, indeed, tell us that we use only a small percentage of our brain's capacity, and the same is true of the heart. Some of the Greek philosophers were indeed hostile to writing and reading, which they regarded as impediments to the full flowering of the human mind. They preferred conversation and dialogue to any other means of mental exchange. Personally, I could not fail to be impressed by the fact that two important turning points in my life were instances when I had nothing to read or to do and was forced to use my own mind and heart to occupy my time.

The first instance took place shortly after the war, when I was a law student at the University of Strasbourg. My parents were still alive and I seized every opportunity to spend my weekends with them in our hometown, about one hundred kilometers from Strasbourg. I used to take the train on Friday evening and return to the university on Monday morning.

One Friday, an unexpected canceling of a lecture gave me the opportunity to catch an early train and I rushed straight from the university to the railroad without returning to my room to fetch my luggage. I was in such a hurry that I did not have the time to buy a book or a magazine. As a result, I found myself sitting alone and empty-handed in a train compartment, without anything to read or do. I had a long journey ahead of me, since the train took almost three hours to reach my hometown. The tracks and equipment had suffered greatly from the war. Most bridges had been blown up and in many places the train had to crawl with utmost caution over temporary structures. What was I to do with my time? I had no notebook, no reading material whatsoever. To look at the scenery would not help either: I loved dearly, it is true, the little Alsatian villages and the peaceful countryside unfolding outside, but I knew them by heart.

All I could do was to let my thoughts wander freely like a butterfly until they found a subject on which they would choose to rest. My mind was thus scanning various thoughts and images when it caught something that had fleetingly retained my attention just before I left the university. It was a poster announcing that the French Association for the United Nations was offering a prize of five thousand francs to the student who would write the best essay on a world government. The award was being offered by Paul Boncour, a former French Premier and a great internationalist and orator.

The question posed in the contest arose persistently in my mind: "What do you think of a world government?" It was as if a brother were addressing the question to me, each time unlocking more little gray cells in my brain:

"Here is your challenge, friend. You were determined to work for peace after all the suffering you saw during the war. You wish to join the United Nations and tell them how to run the world in peace and justice? Well, here is your chance! What indeed is world government? How would you conceive it? Fate addresses this question directly to you, the young underground fighter who has just emerged from the war."

Soon I found myself totally absorbed by the subject, pacing up and down the empty, old-fashioned prewar train compartment. Only the Italian inscription below the window was able to distract my attention, as it had always done since my childhood when my mother explained it to me the first time: *É pericoloso sporgersi* (It is dangerous to lean out). I remember vividly how before the war on that same line, a young classmate of mine had put his head out of the window and had been decapitated by a fast train coming from the other direction.

When I arrived home, it was still early in the day, and I sat down at my typewriter to put my ideas on paper and sent them off. A few weeks later I was informed that I had won Mr. Boncour's prize. The essay was published in the UN Association's review. My dear wife has kept a copy of it and she maintains that my labors in the United Nations have remained faithful to the path outlined in that essay. I have never dared to read it again, afraid as I am to find in it another proof of my idealistic and perhaps unrealistic belief in the progress and goodness of human nature. But I have often wondered what my fate would have been if I had stepped into that train with a stack of textbooks, magazines, or newspapers. My essay opened to me the doors of the United Nations and determined my entire professional life. Therefore, when people sometimes ask me, "How did you enter the United Nations?" I always answer truthfully:

"It all happened because one day I was sitting in a train and had nothing to read."

The second instance took place twenty years later in India, when I attended the first United Nations Conference on Trade and Development, in New Delhi. I was deeply fascinated by that enchanting country, by its people, customs, religions, beliefs, and ways of life. Not only did I read avidly about it, but also, with a small group of UN colleagues, I seized every opportunity to visit on weekends, either by bus, train, or plane, places of interest within reach of New Delhi.

Thus, one Friday afternoon, we took a bus to visit Jaipur, the pink city of Rajastan, one of the three most beautiful cities in the world, together with Venice and Peking, according to ancient travelers.

The bus ride lasted late into the night. As long as daylight prevailed, no one got tired or bored. Our eyes and minds were feasting endlessly on Indian scenery: villages bustling with life, colorful temples and marketplaces, disparate vehicles from the Middle Ages, immobile black water buffaloes immersed in tranquil ponds, camels superbly indifferent to the scenes of poverty unfolding at their feet, magnificent children's faces with the most beautiful eyes on earth, rows of vultures perched on treetops, waiting for the dusk to do their environmental job, and so on and so forth.

When evening came, we had reached the Aravalli Mountains, which emerge from the vast alluvial plain of the Ganges like the back of a prehistoric animal. The day died in a pink and purple glory amid the sudden religious silence of our Hindu travel companions. A long pause was scheduled at Alwar, the capital of a tiger territory and a former seat of a maharaja. The bus stopped at his palace, which had been transformed into a rest house for the weary travelers from New Delhi. Light food and tea were served to the passengers, but the night was too beautiful to remain between four walls. I went out to explore the surroundings of the palace and found myself in a magnificent park at the end of which stood a little temple. Alleys covered with lozenges of white marble shone like phosphorescent arabesques under the full moon. Big shadows in orange trees began to moan in the silence of the night: They were peacocks, the most magnificent of all wild birds of India.

On a terrace near the palace I had noticed an Indian bed, one of those simple wooden structures interlaced with ropes on which the body rests flatly. I seized it and carried it to the middle of the lawn under the flood of the moonlight. I lay down on it, folded my hands under my head, and stared at the deep, dark, velvety sky. The night, the air, and nature were so inebriating that I soon found myself addressing incantations to the stars. It was one of those rare moments in life when one feels detached from earth and part of the universe. The soul seems to quit the body and to lose itself among the stars, while remaining thinly attached to flesh and blood by invisible threads. My mind and heart were filled with dreams of joy. I found myself praying to the Indian gods and goddesses to keep me forever in their enchanted land.

But I was abruptly called back to reality when the bus blew its horn a first time. I returned to the rest house to grab a cup of tea and a sandwich before resuming our long journey. I let myself fall into an armchair and asked a boy to serve me swiftly. While waiting for him, my eyes suddenly caught sight of a ravishing young Indian girl, sitting in an armchair opposite mine. She was dressed in the most beautiful golden sari one can imagine. She had a body and features worthy of a goddess. Her harmonious, intelligent face was enlivened by magnificent, brilliant, black eyes. Her raven blue hair, tightly braided, gave her features a voluptuous sense of nudity, intensely enhanced by deep-red, bulging lips. She was holding a magazine in her hands, which lay immobile on her lap. Her melancholy eyes were lost in some faraway place, as if she were waiting for a prince charming or a young god from heaven. To me she looked indeed like an Indian goddess of love descended on earth in response to my incantations.

I had to tear myself from that enchanting scene when the horn blew for the second time. I had a last, intense look at the lovely apparition and was thinking sadly that I would never see her again. It was one of those poignant moments when one realizes that a precious encounter, a sight of great beauty, a deep human emotion will vanish for all eternity. And the young Indian girl would never know what a storm of feelings she had aroused in me in those few exalted moments.

I climbed back into the bus, and the interminable ride began again through the night. Once in a while a group of people, buffaloes, or vehicles appeared under the headlights, but otherwise there was nothing to see, nothing to do. Most passengers soon fell asleep or were drowsing under the shiplike movements of the old van rushing forward on its bumpy road like a boat moving through a storm. I was crisply awake, perhaps under the effect of the tea. My thoughts and dreams were my companions. As in the train from Strasbourg to Sarreguemines, my mind began to wander until it found a subject of its liking. It did. It found the outline of a love story centering on the young Hindu girl briefly seen at Alwar. I visualized myself as a young diplomat arriving in India, taking the same trip, seeing the ravishing girl in the maharaja's palace, interrupting my voyage, staying at the rest house, talking to her, falling in love with her, and finally marrying her. I could fill such a story with all my love and fascination for India, its past, its traditions, its art and music, its legends and beliefs. I could describe all the beautiful places I had seen. Its central piece would be a love scene under the full moon in the park of Alwar... .

I indeed wrote the novel during my lonely evenings in the Lodhi Hotel in New Delhi. To nourish it I took innumerable travel notes and spared no effort to get well acquainted with Indian customs and traditions. I secured invitations to Indian Vedic weddings in order to observe the ceremony and describe it in my book. The story is not an exciting one. It lacks intrigue and is merely a kind of midsummernight's dream. But it gave me immense pleasure to write, and it anchored in me even more deeply my love for India. It also opened a new period in my life: the beginning of my fondness for writing, which has been a boundless and godsent enchantment for me. "Sima My Love" was my first manuscript and it has engendered many other writings since then. Perhaps indeed my prayer in the park of Alwar did set off a spark between a lovely Indian goddess and me. . . .

Thus, two instances when I had nothing to read or to do were responsible for two of the most important turning points in my life. A book in my hands in the train from Strasbourg or a light in the bus from Alwar to Jaipur might have changed my life entirely and perhaps stifled two of my most precious joys: work for the United Nations and writing.

Many people, I am sure, have had similar experiences in their lives, proving that man's own mind and heart are his greatest friends and treasures. We must use and exercise our wonderful capacities for dreams, creativity, and love, and not lose ourselves entirely in the dreams, sentiments, and creations of others. Each of our lives is a unique miracle that we can bring to full flowering through good care and cultivation.

Of Encouragement

There are immense virtues in encouragement. We must stimulate each other to be good, happy, and fulfilled people.

In my view, Chile has the most beautiful women on earth. This is not so well known abroad, for Chile is a relatively small country located at the extreme rim of South America, isolated from the rest of the world by the high chain of the Andes and the vast Pacific. Many countries, therefore, have never seen any Chileans, except for members of diplomatic missions. However, in North and Latin America, Chilean women are well known and greatly admired. The story goes that when a Chilean woman is announced at a party, the lady of the house asks that her husband be locked up or go into hiding!

I married the first Chilean girl I met in my life. We were both interns at the United Nations in Lake Success in 1948. I came as an essay winner from France, and she was a member of the Chilean diplomatic service. When I saw her for the first time, I was speechless before her beauty. I did not dare dream for a moment that she would ever become my wife. But God and fate were good to me and blessed me with a wonderful romance. If there is something for which I am particularly grateful in life, it is for that love and for the beautiful family that ensued.

Later, when I visited Chile, I could see for myself that the reputation of Chilean women was not exaggerated. I inquired why this was so and heard several theories: their Spanish origin, a possible contribution from the Araucanian Indian stock (their velvety eyes), the climate, and even certain food habits. Chilean women, for example, believe that fish keeps the body slim and that squash has the remarkable property of giving girls beautiful, firm legs. I have seen my wife serve squash to our two girls at least once a week for many years.

I have another theory about the beauty of Chilean women: I believe that the artisans of that beauty are . . . Chilean men! What led me to that finding is a popular Chilean saying that the beauty of flowers is due to the care of the gardener. Chilean men have an admiration and adulation for their women that is unmatched in any other country. Chileans make it a rule to compliment their women on every possible occasion, to pay attention to them, to be sweet, to notice their beauty and efforts at embellishment, to be proud of them, and to be always original and poetic when they talk to them. The common man in the street, the worker (or *roto*, as he is called), is a great master at paying compliments, and Chilean girls and women love to exchange notes on the *piropos* they receive. Chileans abroad often miss these gentle, usually quite delicate and inoffensive remarks of men in the street. I have many examples of them, but I like particularly the following one addressed to my wife when she was working for the Ministry of Foreign Affairs in Santiago: Each day she used to leave her office in the Moneda around noon to have luncheon in a nearby restaurant. Once, workers were digging ditches on the sidewalk. As she was passing by, a workman sitting with his unopened lunch box on his lap said to her:

"*Mijita* [my little one], why are you so late today? Don't you know that I cannot eat before I have seen your beauty?"

Chile is also, to my knowledge, the only country on earth that celebrates the cult of women of a certain age. Chilean men hold the view that a woman is really beautiful only after she has reached forty. They have coined a word for them: the famous *cuarentonas*. As a result, Chilean males have the best of two worlds: young women and girls with their natural beauty, and women in their forties who, in order to live up to their reputation, succeed in remaining beautiful, youthful, slim, cheerful, attractive, well-dressed, and confident in their exquisite charm. How many times have I met Chilean women in that age group who were at the peak of their beauty, untouched and perhaps even enhanced by their numerous maternities.

Doubtless, it also helps that Chileans are great poets at heart. They sing their women, their families, their mountains, their sea, their lakes, their wines, their fruit, their seafood, their origin, their land. They celebrate life. They love life. This passion is their whole secret. Chile has produced some of the greatest poets of this century. Names like Gabriela Mistral and Pablo Neruda belong to the world and are magnificent contributions of Chile to humanity's prestigious ascent. I still remember Gabriela Mistral when she came for the first time to the United Nations, representing Chile in the Commission for Women's Rights in 1952. My wife was her alternate, having won herself considerable fame with her work and book on the legal status of women in Chile. When she introduced me to Gabriela Mistral and told her that I was French, the poetess left us for some distant dream and said:

"When I was a young girl I loved to go to the orchard and listen to the wind. There is nothing more beautiful on earth than wind. The wind talks, sings, and whines. The wind comes from faraway lands where it has touched other brothers and sisters. When I visited your country for the first time, I learned that you had a poet who bore the name of a wind: Mistral. I followed his example and I changed my name to Gabriela Mistral. . . ."

I also remember her saying to my wife, who was expecting her first baby:

"*Mijita*, do not worry too much about women's rights. You bear in yourself the most precious gift on earth: the life of a child. Men will never be our equals, for woman alone is blessed with the miracle of motherhood."

Although Gabriela Mistral never had that joy herself, she later sent my wife a volume of beautiful poems: *Poemas de las Madres* (The Poems of Mothers).

Among many other stories about Chilean poetry, I cannot resist telling the following:

One day a newly appointed Chilean delegate arrived at the United Nations and was attending his first meeting at the General Assembly. He scarcely listened to the debate, did not speak, and missed voting when the moment came. His alternate was a well-known Chilean woman diplomat, Anita Figueroa, who later became the highest-ranking female international civil servant when she was appointed deputy director general of the International Labour Organisation. Sitting behind him, she tried in vain to get him to be attentive and to vote, but he did not react. When the meeting was over, he asked her:

"Why were you so worried, my dear?"

"I am upset because we had specific instructions to vote on that issue."

"But *mijita*, don't you see this heavenly blonde sitting in the seat of Sweden, a true goddess from the skies of the North? How could I pay any attention to a dull debate full of human quarrels when I am blinded by such beauty?"

And he handed her a poem he had written during the meeting. It was entitled: *Aguas claras* (Clear Waters), a most beautiful poem, which became quite famous in Chile.

A great lesson can be drawn from the Chilean example; it relates directly to human affairs and to happiness: There are immense virtues in encouragement. Indeed, to stress beauty engenders beauty. To encourage joy creates joy. To promote peace breeds peace. And the same is true for everything good and everything bad on earth. Once again we encounter the eternal choice between the sunny and the somber sides of life and the wide freedom open to each of us to be either a creator or a destroyer, an agent of beauty, peace, human faith, and happiness or a spreader of conflict, pessimism, immorality, and discontent. St. Paul says with respect to father and son relations: "And you, fathers, do not nag your sons lest they lose heart." One could broaden this statement and say: "And you, humans, do not nag your fellow humans lest they lose heart."

Encouragement rests on faith, and faith is founded on love. Encouragement is a great, powerful instrument of man. Without encouragement, how can a person struggle and progress, how can humanity succeed? For what is true of individuals is also true of col-lectivities. It applies to you and to me, to our families, to our town, to our country, and no less to humanity. Therefore, whenever a campaign is being launched against the United Nations for one reason or another, I say to my audiences:

"Are you not the first to agree that the world is faced with very considerable problems? You also think that the United Nations should help solve these problems. But how can the UN succeed without your faith and encouragement? Too many people do not believe in the UN. They criticize it, lash out at it, call it inefficient and ineffective, and sometimes even hate it when their interests are touched in the slightest. Why don't they love it instead, defend it, encourage it, and give this first godsent instrument for world peace and order a chance to succeed in the face of truly gigantic problems? It is as if my son stood in front of a large ditch and I said to him:

"'Son, do you see this ditch? It is enormous. You must jump over it and help me. My life depends on you.'

"But no sooner than having said that, I would add:

"'But you will not be able to do it. You do not have the strength. You do not have the guts. You are no good. I do not believe in you. You are a weakling, a failure, etc. . . .'

"I ask you: Do you think in all honesty that he will be able to jump over the ditch? Certainly not, unless he possessed a tremendous belief in himself. But how many people have the strength to succeed entirely on their own, without encouragement and against the odds of the disbelief of others? One must encourage and not discourage those who are fighting for peace and good on earth."

This is the lesson we can draw from the intelligent attitude of Chilean men toward their women. It is the modern and eternal version of Pygmalion, the sculptor who created a statue of such beauty that she became alive under his hands in response to his love. It is the story of the creator and of creation. It is also the story of the world. In order to model a happy and beautiful world, we must believe in it; we must work at it; we must be in love with it; we must reach out for the highest levels of peace, justice, beauty, and happiness; we must encourage each other in this task, individual to individual, nation to nation, race to race, culture to culture, continent to continent. Nothing but happiness is good enough for the genial and proud human race on planet Earth. Maximum peace, beauty, and happiness and not maximum economic welfare must be the objectives of the coming World Renaissance.

The beauty of flowers is due to the care of the gardener. The beauty of the world will depend on the care of its gardeners. Let us therefore all become loving gardeners of the world. If, like Pygmalion, we use the full power of our heart to engender peace, justice, beauty, and happiness, a miracle will occur: There will be peace, justice, beauty, and happiness on our planet.

Of Meditation and Prayer

*Through prayer and silent contemplation we allow entry into
ourselves of the deeper streams of life and are recompensed with
harmony, serenity, and bliss.*

Since childhood I have observed that my richest, happiest, and mentally most rewarding hours are those just before sunrise. A normal
day without excesses and a good night of sleep are invariably followed
by a high intensity of dreams toward the end of the night and by an
early awakening of the mind. At five or six o'clock in the morning,
when my family is still asleep, I find myself resting in bed, mind and
body completely awake and relaxed, without any physical or mental
distractions whatsoever. In this state of rest, ideas, images, and
thought associations begin to dance in my brain like young mice in a
deserted house. It is a most interesting spectacle: I can distinctly
observe the birth, paths, speeds, hesitations, collisions, adaptations,
crisscrossings, and twirlings of ideas spontaneously engendered in
my mind during these subtle, silent morning hours. The process is
not "thinking," which I would associate with system and effort. My
body and brain are not in any sense actors: They seem to be merely
"visited" by ideas that find in them a hospitable ground for their play.
These thoughts have a life of their own, unrelated to my being.
Aspects suddenly become clear that had escaped me during daytime.
Basic truths about life, people, and the world are revealed to me in
fleeting, evanescent moments of intense clarity. And still the brain is
totally at rest, motionless, effortless, like a peaceful sea filled with
information and knowledge about the world — its past, present, and
future. The surface of that sea is animated by ripples that I can

observe as if I were detached from my body. My brain is watching itself, capable of self-inversion, like a motor that would be able to observe its own functioning! Most of my actions, doings, writings, talks, and initiatives during the day are thus being bred at dawn in a strange, self-engendered, autonomous process.

This state of mind lasts for about an hour. There is not a detail of it that I would forget, so intense are its markings. Anything "seen" or perceived during these early moments becomes an intimate part of myself and will reappear at the proper time during the day.

Then I rise, go to another room, and write down the thoughts that have come to me, in letters, essays, speeches, and action proposals. This lasts for another hour until normal day-life begins, with one's integration into the animated, observable world of sounds, images, feelings, doings, and agitations. The mysterious, silent morning hours give way to the contests of people, ideas, dreams, media, machines, and institutions that make up the total fabric of diurnal life. The brain captures all this, adds it *pêle-mêle* to its fund of knowledge and doubts, lets it settle down, digests it during the night, and the following morning the tranquil surface waves are observable again, ready to be seen by the total human entity, which thus remains endlessly immersed through its senses in the restless streams of life.

At one point, prayer comes quite naturally to my lips, first as a feeling of gratitude for being alive, for having the privilege of another day, for being "resurrected" and for possessing so much health, family, employment, and a passion for life — then in the form of one of those simple, beautiful prayers that my mother taught me when I was a child, and finally by seeing my humble but precious place in the total order of things presided over by a force and destiny that I was told to call God and to profoundly revere. At that moment everything falls into place. I am happy, serene, full of gratitude. Everything makes sense. I have no problems, fears, or worries. I feel in my mind, heart, and flesh the plenitude of cosmic peace and order.

This has invariably been my pattern since early childhood, interrupted only by one rich and important variation: Sometimes I get up, attracted by the prospect of a beautiful sunrise, and I lose myself in the silent glory of the day's resurrection. To watch the sun rise behind the majestic chain of the Alps, the Andes, or the Himalayas, above the Moghol tombs of India or the mosques of Istanbul, the ocher hills of Cyprus, the glorious Hudson, or Manhattan's silent skyscrapers count among the most ecstatic moments of my life. Like Goethe's Faust, I am tempted to exclaim, *"Hier bin Ich Mensch, hier darf Ich's sein"* (Here I am human, here I am free) . . . free to embrace the beauty of the world, allowed to touch the veil of the universe, to live moments of supreme ecstasy.

I never paid much attention to these daybreak states of mind. I simply accepted and enjoyed them as a natural functioning of my being, and they helped me greatly to achieve self fulfillment and happiness. I did not establish any connections between them and "meditation" until I knew U Thant. He was meditating every morning before coming to the United Nations, in order, as he told me, "to set things straight and put one's daily life into proper perspective." I noticed that this gave him a great peace of mind, inner strength, and immunity from irrational mental and physical moods. I was working personally during the day on the basis of the surface ripples observed at dawn, initiating actions and proposals under the instructions of my brain's diagnosis. U Thant was more deeply immersed in spirituality and less inclined to believe that the world could be changed. He used to say: "The West is too restless, too impatient, too insatiable. The Orient is too meditative, too philosophical, not progressive enough. Humanity must seek a proper blend between the two approaches." But he never got around to talking to me about meditation, a subject on which I had confessed to him my total ignorance. Even during my stay in India, where I fell in love with so many aspects of that country's life, I never really felt attracted to a practice that, as distinct from religion and prayer, seemed limited to an elite and had no real roots in the great mass of the people. Of course, like everyone else, I was fascinated by the sight of holy men sitting near the temples, their intelligent faces lost in stillness and eternity, or by the black-bearded, hairy hermits emerging at mealtime from their rock caves in the hills above the Ganges in Richikech, totally deprived of material possessions except for a piece of yellow cloth wrapped around their loins. I had curiosity and respect for such men but made no effort to find out what occupied their minds and hearts and how they reached these states.

It was a young American student from Iowa who acquainted me for the first time with meditation. I had delivered a speech on world population and resources at Iowa State University at Ames under the auspices of the university's Institute on World Affairs. My optimistic assessment of the future irritated a professor of ecology who had been teaching the advent of cataclysms to his students. He took violent issue with me and I was somewhat embarrassed by the acidity and bitterness of his attack, when a young man arose and took my defense in very moving and eloquent terms. There was in his intervention a sense of ascent of humankind that I found very beautiful and encouraging. After the meeting he came to see me, handed me a big volume with golden imprints, and said to me:

"You have the right heart and inclination toward people and the world. May I pray you to have a look at this book. Take it to New York, read it at a moment of peace, ponder over it, and someday I will contact you at the United Nations to discuss it with you.

Back in my hotel, when I discovered that it was the catalogue of a university called "Maharishi International University," I was tempted to throw it into the wastebasket. But the honest, radiant face of the young man came back to my mind and in deference to his idealism I kept the volume and read it in the airplane. I was fascinated by it. I learned how meditation functioned and what it did for the fulfillment of the human person. I discovered that I had been meditating for years without knowing it. I did it more than a few minutes every morning, letting the process run out its normal course for as long as my nature dictated and feeling no inclination to repeat it in the evening, which is the weakest period of my day.

I learned many interesting facts about the process and its effects. It leads apparently to increased stability, faster reactions, greater perceptual ability, improved learning capacity, better job performance, decreased anxiety and blood pressure, reduced use of alcohol and tobacco, relief from insomnia, improved resistance to disease, and more generally increased self-fulfillment and enjoyment of life. The method is applied as a background for all the university's teachings, from biology and sciences to education and political economy.

I was obviously impressed by what I read and thankful to the young Iowan for having given me the book. As I was looking out of the aircraft into the deep blue sky and over the vast fields of the American Midwest, cherished memories came back to me: I saw myself as a child, lying in my bed in my hometown on the border of France with Germany, listening to the sound of the rain falling on the roof; I remembered the divine moments of early Mass in our old majestic church, the angelic songs of the nuns, the Latin chants and prayers, and the moaning sound of an old organ played by an invalid; I relived my deep communion with God and the universe when I watched the dawning of the day in the hills of Auvergne; I saw in my mind rows of Hindus praying and kneeling before the sun god Surya as he rose above the sacred waters of the Ganges; I could hear in my heart the crystalline voice of a young woman singing her joy to the sky while hanging her children's clothes in the hills of Spain above the golden bay of Benidorm. . . . Be it through meditation, prayer, silence, or song, the miracles of life and resurrection are widely open to each of us every day of God's creation. We are part of eternity and of the universe. It cannot be otherwise. We may be blinded to this truth by our narrow "interests" and have our eyes glued to the ground, but prayer, meditation, and the silent contemplation of nature, reborn each day under the sun's glory, bring us in direct communion with God and the universe. Prayer and meditation are two of the surest and quickest ways to happiness. Through them we reduce our petty arrogance and personal barriers against the streams of life. Letting these streams flow unimpeded through the miraculous point of perception that we are, we feel the greatness of all things, thoughts, sentiments, and dreams. We see everything in harmony and proportion. We are aggrandized beyond measure. We become fully human, fully alive, fully free.

It is strange that people from the East — maharishis, yogis, seers, Buddhists, and others — have to come and teach us afresh what we already knew; for we have been taught to pray morning and evening, to communicate with God, to respect life, to love our brethren, to keep our bodies, minds, and souls clean. We know about morality, ethics, and the supremacy of the spirit. But how many people in the West dare to proclaim, like these new magi from the East, that prayer helps them set things straight, that their daily lives are inseparable from religion, that life is religion, ethics, morality, cleanliness, love, understanding, and gratitude? What other life is worth living? Is it not time to reassert in the West these simple but fundamental truths and restore the supremacy of ethics and spirituality over the intellectualism and rationalism of our time? There is more in heaven and on earth than in our industries and sciences. Prayer and meditation are two of the first revived ancient steps toward a new age in which humans will use again their wonderful powers of heart and soul to live fuller and happier lives than ever before.

Leonardo's Notebook

Take the time to observe yourself and the surrounding world, and write it all down.

One day I learned that a book entitled *Leonardo da Vinci's Advice to Artists*,[1] by Emery Kelen, had been published. When I joined the UN as a young staff member, I had been introduced to Kelen, a famous caricaturist who was particularly prominent during the League of Nations when European and American newspapers were still carrying, almost daily, drawings and caricatures of well-known people. I had had occasion to see his work at the UN in New York, and in Geneva at the Restaurant Bavaria, which displays one of the most remarkable collections of caricatures extant. Whenever I met Kelen in the corridors of the UN, I greeted him with respect, but during all those years I never engaged in a conversation with him. Tall, his shoulders curved as if he were carrying a heavy load, his deep, penetrating eyes firmly riveted in vast, somber sockets under thick, protruding eyebrows, a head cut to order for a strong, reflective, and observant personality, he was not the type of man I would have walked up to, saying hello and asking him to have a beer with me. But when I read about his book, I decided to call him and ordered copies for my daughters, who are great art lovers and good artists themselves.

He brought the books to my office, and when he saw me surrounded by sculptures and paintings, he launched into a conversation that counts among the most fascinating I have had. He told me of his passion for the human face and how he had become a caricaturist.

[1]Nashville, Tenn.: Thomas Nelson, Inc., 1974.

"I was a soldier in the Austro-Hungarian army and was engaged in one of the most gruesome battles of World War I, at Isonzo. I decided I would work for peace if I survived. After the war, I studied law and went to Geneva with the intention of joining the staff of the League of Nations. One day, in a doctor's office, I perused a book on the human face by a certain Kretschmer. I borrowed it and read it with fascination. It changed the course of my life. The study, observation, understanding, and drawing of the human face became a passion, a real obsession with me. There is not a book on the subject, from passages in the old Greek and Latin authors to contemporary works from East and West, that I have not read. What I learned and observed about the human face is all consigned to a book that I hope to publish someday."

And he spoke about Aristotle's *Treatise on Physiognomy*, the Code of Hammurabi, Lavater, Giacomo della Porta, Kretschmer, and Sheldon, all great names associated with the study of the human face.

"The subject will again become important," he said, "in view of the role of television. Candidates are elected for their looks and their faces, and people are right in trusting their instinct. Doctors are locked up in their anatomical science, which does not explain the relations among the human face, the external world, and the internal soul. Even Chinese acupuncture is only a determination of points. The human face is something prodigious, insufficiently studied. I have collected over one hundred books dealing with the subject and I still feel that we have barely scratched the surface of a science that will involve genetics, biochemistry, psychology, and other fields of knowledge."

I myself had always been fascinated by the human face, and I commented

"Whenever a person is sitting in front of me, I instinctively begin to analyze his character, inner motives, dreams, moods, and ambitions on the basis of his facial traits. To me the eyes are the most telling feature. There is a world in the eyes of a human being.

Eyes are so frighteningly full that I can seldom bear to look into them for more than a few seconds. Another important aspect is telepathy. I sometimes have the impression that invisible feelers extending from my being are exploring, testing, and mapping out the telepathic projections of the other person. I am astonished by the minutiae, intensity, and quasi-palpable reality of these invisible contacts, while the two people may be speaking about something entirely different."

He remarked:

"This is not surprising. Your extrasensory capacity derives from the mesomorphic or round shape of your head."

And to my astonishment he very accurately described the main traits of my character and outlook toward life!

"People with the shape of your head are usually successful businessmen, and if you were not sitting behind this desk at the United Nations, you would have probably made a fortune."

He went on explaining the character of several people, distinguishing among those with elongated, thin heads, like De Gaulle, and those with spherical heads and round faces, like Benjamin Franklin and Churchill. My mind in the meantime was wandering to India, where I had learned of the importance of Samudrika Sastra, or the study of the appearance of a person. From very early times, the Hindus have evolved a system of foretelling the character and fate of a person from his appearance, gait, manner of speech and, above all, certain characteristics of the body, especially the head and face. In interviewing candidates for appointments to positions of trust and seeing young men or women with a view to matrimony in ancient and medieval India, services of experts in Samudrika Sastra were secured, and often their verdict was accepted as final. Today, the ancient art is still used by orthodox Hindus in some marriages.

Kelen then spoke about the other great love of his life: Leonardo da Vinci.

"I wanted to know what Leonardo had to say about the human face and I spent countless days deciphering and studying his writings. In the course of my investigations I discovered Leonardo's children's stories, which had never been published. My find earned me a literary prize in Europe in the 1930s."

I could have listened for hours to this extraordinary man. Here was someone to my liking, a being who had an endless passion for the puzzles and mysteries of life and of the human person. Alas, after a while he rose and said:

"I am so sorry I have to leave, but it is my last day in New York. I am returning to Vienna, where I will retire and continue to write books. My only regret is that we met so late and that I discovered only now how much we have in common!"

I shared the same feeling. Seldom had anyone left such a deep impression on me in such a short time.

I read his book on Da Vinci. It was my first encounter with Leonardo's famous notebooks. I learned that Leonardo always carried a notebook hanging from his belt, on which he wrote any interesting observation or thought that struck his mind. He left several thousands of pages of the most fascinating notes a human being has ever written, interspersed with drawings, inventions, and endless fantasies. Kelen writes:

"His interests dwelt on just about anything under the sun. In one modern compilation of these notes, I have counted seventynine different subjects on forty-nine pages, among them a comparison of the movements of the tides with the passage of air in the lungs and observations on the increase in the size of the pupils in the eyes of an owl, a man, and a cat; on the problem of squaring the circle; on how the earth's surface is increased by the growth of vegetation; on what the wings of a flying machine ought to be like; and on the measurements of a Sicilian horse.

"Such random scribblings sketch out for us the musings of an almost transcendent mind; he wrote on art, physiology, philosophy, hydrography, ethics, and morality, and sometimes his ramblings seem to spill over the edges of ordinary thinking, so that they cannot be understood at all. Such dissertations appear side by side with a recipe for perfume, with household accounts, with expenditures for the funeral of a woman, Caterina, or with the cold and stark: "At 7:00 A.M. on Wednesday, July 9, 1504, Ser Piero da Vinci, my father, notary to the Podestá, died. He was eighty years old and left ten sons and two daughters."

Leonardo's habit confirmed my instinct for another recipe of happiness that I had adopted in my life, namely, the custom of keeping a diary. As a student it had struck me that the renowned French author Montesquieu, a judge at the Parliament of Bordeaux, always carried slips of paper in his pockets, on which he wrote his thoughts on the human condition and on his time. These notes provided the basis for his famous book *The Spirit of Laws*, which became the ideological guide for the American and French revolutions and for much of the political thinking of our time. Numerous other authors throughout the centuries relied on notebooks and diaries as foundations for their writings.

One day, sitting in a United Nations meeting in Geneva, I became so bored with the divergent views and squabblings of the participants that my eyes and mind began to concentrate on the movements of a squirrel in a tree, on the flights of birds in the sky, and on the play of sun rays in a jug of water on the conference table. I jotted down my observations, and in the evening, when I read them, I felt somehow enriched in my experience of life. Ever since, I have been taking daily notes. I scribble them down at any moment: in the night during a period of insomnia — sometimes catching the tail end of a dream, at dawn, at a meeting, in the office, in an airplane, in a train, on a boat, and even in the street if an interesting thought that might never return crosses my mind. This heaven-sent habit has immensely enriched my life. It has forced me to be more observant of the functioning of my being, senses, brain, and heart in relation to the surrounding world, as well as of the thoughts, dreams, feelings, and aspirations of others. Since man is part of the total knowledge, thoughts, and feelings of the whole human race, he can thus learn vastly more about the human condition than by reading voluminous books. I found that an idea was never *my* idea, but that it belonged to a collective brain in which all humans partake. I was only catching it at the fleeting moment when it visited me. I lost my identity and saw myself in communion with all other humans. I became a fuller and happier person and gained a better command over my intellectual and sentimental abilities.

Also, writing being a process of conservation, my daily notes engraved more deeply into my memory what crossed my eyes and mind as a personally felt truth or reality. I had the impression that my life was not "lost," that it acquired more meaning. Whenever I stop taking notes for a few days, I become ill-humored and feel like someone who is wasting his life. I discovered also how difficult it is to remember and reconstruct what one did, felt, or thought only a few days ago.

It confirmed me in my belief that man's most precious good is life itself. To better observe, to see more sharply, to embrace life more avidly, to understand others more generously, to think farther into the future and the past, to see humanity and the world as part of the flow of time, became important building blocks of my happiness and passion for life. Each annotation, thought, and image elevated me a notch higher in my understanding and marvel at the riches of life and of our planet. An endless process of trial and error, of constant correction of my thoughts and behavior brought me closer to a serene and satisfactory comprehension of life.

My daily notes thus provided me with endless materials for speeches and writings on the state of the world and the human condition. I no longer needed to exert any great efforts or consult ponderous books. The main elements were all in my mind, collected, classified, and stored as they came along during my daily work, my travels, my dealings with other people, and as answers to my endless interrogations. My inhibitions disappeared. I was able to deliver on short notice a speech on almost any subject, while in earlier times it would have taken me weeks of cumbersome preparation. And people liked my speeches because they were deeply felt. They made sense out of the complexity and the confusion. I had a confident view of human evolution. My vision sounded right because it was the fruit of genuine observation and came from the innermost part of my soul. I was able to relate everything to a central cause, to a point of convergence, to what seemed to me the sense and beauty of the miracle of life.

I could say infinitely more about the marvelous harvest of self-fulfillment and profit one derives from taking daily notes, especially if they are not to be published or read by anyone else. To prove my point, I will tell the following anecdote, which sheds an interesting light on the subject.

One summer, my wife and I were participating in an international conference in Europe. The meeting gave occasion to several receptions and enjoyable excursions. My wife struck up a friendship with a wonderful young woman, the wife of one of the participants. One evening I had the privilege of sitting next to the young woman at a dinner-dance party in a charming, ancient village. Good food, generous wine, and a lively local band were stirring our blood. We danced together. She took her shoes off and twirled around in graceful and impassioned movements, offering a perfect image of youth and happiness. We talked profusely. She told me that she was in love with joy and beauty and that she did not want to hear of anything else. She abhorred many aspects of diplomatic life as being a waste of time. "For example, I came to this dinner because I knew that I would enjoy myself, but I refused to show up at luncheon because I thought I would be infinitely happier lying on the beach, listening to the wonderful sounds of nature, and feeling the warmth of the sun caress my body."

She spent at least three hours a day writing: "Nobody can take these precious moments away from me. I write early in the morning and consign on paper anything that comes to my mind, especially what I dreamed during the night. It is all so fascinating. The more I write, the more I discover the beauty of life. I am convinced that I belong to a universal soul that encompasses all things on earth and in the universe. In my dreams I am visiting other planets, and I write down what I saw and felt. I see myself resuscitated in other beings and on other worlds. Death no longer seems to exist for me. Life, since I began writing, has become so dear, so wonderful, so precious."

I looked at her with astonishment. I thought I was listening to myself. Then she added in a subdued voice this strange comment:

"I have a very intelligent doctor. He insists that I must write at least three hours a day and that I hand him each week the result of my work."

When my wife and I regained our hotel we commented on the evening. She too had been totally enthralled by her new friend, and their common zest for life had brought them very close together. Then, after a moment of hesitation, she looked at me and said:

"Do you know that this wonderful woman, blessed with youth, beauty, wealth, intelligence, and children knows . . . that she is going to die? She has an incurable sickness."

I was thunderstruck with disbelief and rebellion. Now her remark took on its full meaning: "I have a very intelligent doctor. . . ." Yes, indeed, she had a very intelligent doctor who, by requiring her to write about herself was able to make her find temporary oblivion and extract the maximum she could from her remaining days. I shuddered at the thought of the power contained in the will for life, even in the face of death. I could not think of any better illustration to prove what immeasurable profit can be derived from observing oneself and the surrounding world and writing it all down.

Of Self-restraint and Exuberance

Both self-restraint and exuberance can lead to happiness.

A question concerning happiness that I have never been able to resolve is the degree to which a human being should exteriorize or, on the contrary, curb his feelings. I have seen cases when the two opposite behaviors were entirely justified and formed part of a consistent philosophy of self-fulfillment. I have known others where a middle course was no less successful. An individual's physiology doubtless plays a cardinal role, but the question is infinitely more complex, since man is deeply conditioned by codes of behavior instilled in him by family, religion, education, political regimes, culture, ancestry, wealth, and more recently by transnational factors. This is a vast and important subject, which will play a determining role in future world order and to which little attention has been paid so far. All I can do is approximate it by narrating the following anecdotes.

Examples of two totally different behaviors were given to me by U Thant, the former Secretary General of the UN, a Buddhist and a Burmese, and by my wife, a Chilean diplomat of Spanish origin.

U Thant was probably the most superb example of self-control one can imagine. I never saw him lose his temper, burst out, change color, be impatient, irritated, critical, superior, accusatory, shift responsibilities, pass the buck, dominate, boss around, talk behind the backs of others, etc. He had none of these bad habits with which Western man is so amply endowed. It was a puzzle, albeit a miracle to me, that someone could live such a self-disciplined and tightly contained emotional life. There was something extremely nice, reassuring, good, and warm about his attitude. It was not the English phlegm that often culminates in some kind of superiority, coldness, and displaced wit that so irritates foreigners. His kindness and serenity proceeded from deep ethical and spiritual values. U Thant was simply behaving in thought, speech, and action the way Buddha had taught his followers to behave, so that they may find serenity in a world marked by tensions, greed, and desire.

He once told me this story, which illustrates the strict Buddhist education he had received:

"One day, when I was eighteen, my father took me to an English boxing match in Rangoon. I watched the spectacle throughout and when it ended, as we went home, my father said to me: "Son, I am very proud of you. I have observed you during the entire event and I saw you express a slight emotion only twice. You have followed my teachings well and I am satisfied with the result I have just seen. You have really learned to control yourself.""

This explains why, many years later, when the tragic news of the sudden death in a traffic accident of his only son in Burma was brought to him, U Thant merely remarked: "Oh! what grief it will be for my poor wife." He kept his emotions to himself and to a minimum, firmly believing that birth and death are two phases of the same process and that death is followed by rebirth as naturally as birth is followed by death.

Such was U Thant, the first Buddhist and first Asian Secretary General of the United Nations, who for ten years presided with calm and composure over the contests among unruly nations.

At home I had the diametrically opposed example of my Chilean wife, to whom exteriorization, music, song, flamenco, discussion, passion, dance, laughter, and tears are as necessary as bread and fresh air. I could list as many aspects of her exuberance as I could of U Thant's self-restraint. The following story shows the contrast with U Thant:

When we got married, we went for our honeymoon to Mexico. For both of us it was our first visit to that enchanting land. For my wife it was also the first time she visited a country where bullfights were authorized. In her country, Chile, such fights were prohibited, but her Spanish father had told her endless nostalgic stories about *corridas*, and she possessed an encyclopedic knowledge about them, without ever having seen one in reality.

One Sunday we went to a program that had been recommended to us as promising to be particularly outstanding. Knowing very little about the sport, I found it crude and cruel, and I could well understand why it was prohibited in so many countries. But my wife knew all the rules and refinements and she could appreciate the infinite variations of what went on in the ring. For her it was the greatest spectacle on earth. She was commenting loudly, rising to her feet, shouting bravos and *olés*, joining her encouragements to those of the thunderous Mexicans, entranced by the calculated, graduated risks of the toreador, waving the new white straw hat she had just bought in New York for the Easter Parade. When the fight was over, the bull killed, and the torero allowed to cut an ear, my wife could not resist any longer: Jumping once more on her feet, she threw her new and beautiful hat into the arena as a tribute to the toreador. She then sat down, relaxed, sighed, smiled radiantly, remembered me, took my hand, dug her nails into it, and said that she was the happiest woman on earth. If U Thant's father had witnessed that scene, he would have suffered a heart attack, whereas her own father would have embraced her, hugged her, and probably left the arena, arm in arm with her, forgetting completely about me!

The life philosophy of my wonderful Hispanic wife has always been to "get it out of the system." If your day has been hard, if you have problems, talk them out with someone, raise your voice, silence your worries through song and laughter, dance them to death, do not keep them to yourself, and if you are a woman, cry a little once in a while. The images of folkloric dances and of Zorba the Greek come forthwith to mind. They are sound and simple popular ways to get rid of tensions and pent-up feelings. To her American friends who are spending fortunes on psychological and psychiatric treatment, she always says: "Sing, dance, laugh, talk, pray, sit down in a church, confess to a priest, and talk to God and thank him for all the good things you have. And if all this does not help, go and buy yourself a new hat!" Her own practice of these good precepts has blessed me with a happy and most adorable companion.

Who holds the truth? U Thant or my wife? I cannot tell. Each individual has his own ways of happiness and is free to choose from the immense reservoir of customs, philosophies, practices, beliefs, and recipes that human evolution has produced since the beginnings of mankind. The doctors, however, would probably give a little edge to my wife, for they always felt that U Thant's strict retention of problems was the cause of his ulcers.

To work for peace and world order can indeed be a very frustrating profession, fraught with many tensions. When I was a young UN official, I used to go to one of the playlands at Times Square to shoot out my frustrations at clay pipes, roaring bears, and processions of peaceful, white metal ducks, which fell with a resounding and extremely satisfying sound. I have often jokingly stated that such a shooting gallery should be installed in one of the basements of the UN as a nerve calmer for peacemakers!

The human race has its moods and tensions too, like an individual, and war is all too often the outcome. As humanity advances toward higher levels of evolution, greater provision must be made for the outlet of pent-up emotions through more world sport, world art, world folklore, and world festivities. One should not underestimate the role played by the United Nations in defusing and reducing world tensions. I wonder what our planet would look like if the United Nations were not around to be the first shock absorber, safety lid, and verbal shooting gallery for the innumerable tensions that constantly arise among nations and groups of people.

Of Laughter

A day without laughter is a lost day.

If one remembers that the human body is made of trillions of cells, of a universe of atoms, of miles of vessels, of thousands of intricate mechanisms, automatic clocks, and delicate computers, all bound together by a marvelous, still unexplained force called "life," then indeed laughter, that strange cascade of spasms that shakes the entire human being, becomes a rather prodigious phenomenon.

I have always been intrigued by laughter and sympathetic to people who had a sense of humor. For me a day without laughter is a lost day. From childhood on, I loved to smile and to laugh all by myself. I remember how astonished my father used to be when he visited me in my room on the highest floor of the house:

"Son, I hear you laugh, I hear you whistle. When do you work? How can you study under such conditions?"

"I whistle while I work and I scarcely notice it. I laugh because I am happy. It sets the rhythm of my soul. I am glad to be alive and to learn so many fascinating things about our incredible world. I am happy to feel the pulses of my heart and the musings of my mind. I am happy because there is so much fun and joy in the miracle of life. Sometimes I feel like a god."

Of all the members of my family, I preferred those who had a sense of humor, who felt that life was beautiful, and who did not take the daily chores too seriously. They had sunshine and brilliance in their eyes. They looked youngest and lived longest. I liked also the jesters or joke tellers, those very special individuals of whom there was at least one in every village. They were invited to all family reunions: baptisms, first Communions, weddings, and sometimes even funerals. Youngsters like me learned from them the art of story-telling. I loved it also when my father came home in the evening and told us the latest jokes he had heard in the pub. I wonder today how we would have withstood Nazi occupation had it not been for the constant flow of jokes about their arrogance and stupidity.

I have also learned during my life that laughter is a potent stimulant to health. I once knew a famous stomach surgeon who used laughter as a cure for ulcers and other stomach ailments. His clinic was equipped with a projection room in which hilarious movies were shown to his patients. Norman Cousins once told me that at one point in his life he laughed his way out of a supposedly crippling disease. In the Soviet Union, hospital wards are equipped with bottles of laughing gas, Soviet doctors having discovered that laughter is a potent painkiller and an adjuvant of the healing process of heart diseases. It is perhaps for the same reason that at the funeral meals I attended as a boy, the village joke teller often made people drink and laugh in order to relieve their pain. His performance usually began with the statement that the deceased was looking at us from heaven and did not want us to mourn him but to rejoice at being all together.

All my life I have memorized and collected jokes from various lands and cultures. These jokes never cease to fascinate me. The same jokes my father told us about the French and the Germans reappeared later at the United Nations about Arabs and Jews. The sociology of humor must be a very fascinating subject of study. Every time I visit a new country, I stop in a bookstore and ask for books of jokes. My highest mark goes to southern France, where I once left a bookstore with a whole shopping bag of good humor books and magazines. When I judge a person, I always attach greatest importance to sense of humor. All great people I have known had a deep sense of humor. It is almost a foolproof device for detecting greatness. A man who takes himself too seriously is seldom really a great man. He is lacking something very fundamental. Einstein, De Gaulle, Churchill, Nehru, U Thant all had a great sense of humor. When I met Albert Schweitzer for the first time, in New York, upon learning that I was from Alsace-Lorraine, he forthwith asked me with a twinkle in his eyes: "Do you know the latest joke about the Alsatian who fell into the Rhine? . . ."

A sense of humor can even render a person attractive. I will never forget a diplomatic dinner party at which I met one of the ugliest women I had ever seen in my life. Her features were so unpleasing that scarcely anyone spoke to her. At coffee time, she suddenly began telling jokes and soon thereafter everyone was spellbound at her feet. The rest of the evening was hers. We had forgotten how unattractive she was. Her inner joy and good humor illumined her entire personality. When we said good-bye, I caught myself thinking that it might not be disagreeable to be married to such a person.

Another woman, however, once cast a severe shadow over my admiration for sense of humor. She said:

"The only thing I object to is your enthrallment with jokes. In psychology I learned that jokes are the expression of an inborn sense of fear, insecurity, and aggression. Jokes ridicule the poor, the stupid, the naive, and the helpless. They are always cruel to someone. It hurts me, therefore, to see you enjoy jokes so much."

This remark disturbed me greatly. Perhaps indeed my inclination for jokes was unhealthy and abnormal. Was I at countercurrent with modern civilization? For example, I noticed that less and less people laughed in New York City. In my suburban train to Manhattan, whenever someone laughs, all heads turn in shocking disapproval. Usually it is a recently immigrated Caribbean or Latino who breaks the sacrosanct silence required by the reading of the New York *Times*. Sometimes I believe that vending machines of laughing gas would be a good business in New York.

But later I was fortunate to discover in a French political review a fascinating article, "Humor and Nonviolence," which reassured me completely. It reviewed the views and thoughts of all great psychologists and philosophers on the subject and concluded that humor was one of the highest expressions of liberty. There is apparently a close correlation between humor and the knowledge of oneself. Humor is a constant challenge and irritant to the cloak of seriousness with which every power group in this world disguises its attempts at supremacy, monopoly, and domination. Freud considered humor to be the highest expression of psychic defenses. In his view it spared people of emotions such as anger, disgust, and fear. Humor, according to him, is the self-affirmation of the individual in whatever situation he might find himself.

These views were a revelation to me. They supported my own observations that jokes are usually directed at the holders of power and wealth, at people who take themselves too seriously and try to oppress others under all kinds of rational or sacrosanct pretenses. Thus jokes always flourish in dictatorships and strong regimes. They make the oppressed feel better, they give them a sense of liberty, however tiny it might be. Furthermore, jokes are an admirable instrument for reducing tensions. How many times, in UN meetings, have I seen tensions mount between delegates or officials representing different interests and positions. Dead serious, with all the might of their intelligence, they exaggerate their case, fortify their positions, and escalate their arguments. One can feel the physical tension mount in the room. Onlooking parties remain silent, dismayed by the recurrence of the old human game. But invariably all that is needed to defuse the tension is a good joke by the president. Things immediately return to normal. Everybody, including the protagonists, is relieved, and the meeting can return to its normal pace. Jokes are thus an important instrument of diplomacy. Outsiders are often shocked by the ease with which jokes are told at the UN. Their image of world diplomacy is usually so serious. In reality, humor speaks well for the sense of liberty and self-criticism in a place where every conceivable game of power, interest, and self-glorification is being played. Only humor and common sense can help deflate the old, mystifying, Machiavellian game.

I thus learned that for the tenants of pessimism, jokes and humor are proof of the morbid, sickly, and anguished attitudes of humans toward life, and that for optimists they are proof of the basic joy and inborn sense of liberty in human nature. Of course, I rank myself with the latter.

When in the UN someone complains about life, the response is usually: "Remember the joke of the man who always said: It could be worse . . ." This truly represents a great life philosophy, for indeed, except for death, it usually could be infinitely worse.

A Secret of Youth

Happiness irradiates and makes you look younger.

One morning I was walking to the United Nations when I caught up with a lady who has been working for the UN for many years and with whom I have an occasional exchange of thoughts. She said to me: "I hesitate to put this question to a man, but curiosity compels me to: Why is it that you look so young? You seem to me younger than ever. I believe you will never retire. What is your secret? I observed you the other day and I asked myself: What makes him look so young, so happy? Could it be satisfaction with your job?"

I answered: "Yes, it is just sheer happiness and the joy of being allowed to partake in the beauty and wonders of the world. You see, about ten years ago, having reached my forties, I resolved to stop believing in current ideas. I stopped reading books and stuffing myself with the pessimistic views of others. I turned to myself and relied on my own eyes, brain, and heart to judge life and the world. I observed the functioning of my own being in relation to the surrounding world. I found again the beauty of the world and the happiness of my adolescence. Perhaps my recovered internal joy shows on my face and creates the illusion of youth."

She said: "So I was right. You do have a secret. It is happiness that does that to you."

We had arrived at the UN in the meantime, said good-bye to each other, and took our respective elevators. Several months later I met again the same lady. She looked old and broken, and when I addressed her, I saw tears upwell in her eyes. She said:

"I have lost my husband and I am unable to overcome my grief. I have no children and family left on earth. I am all alone. I barely eat. I cannot sleep. I am taking pills and am on the advice of a psychiatrist. This has now lasted for almost five months and it is not getting any better. Can you help me?"

I invited her for a cup of coffee and I told her two stories from the lives of Abbé Pierre and Mother Teresa. Realizing that I had given two Catholic examples to someone of Jewish faith, I added:

"Go and see your rabbi. Talk to him. Ask him if you can be of help to someone. You think you are the most miserable person on earth, but your condition may look like paradise to cripples, poor, and moribunds. Your rabbi will certainly help you. If nothing else works, I always turn to my religion and to its pastors: They have thousands of years of experience in dealing with life, suffering, and death. They are devoted to helping others. It is their profession, the reason for their existence. They had invented the confessional long before the psychiatrists thought of the couch. Take my advice, give up your pills and psychiatrist and see your rabbi."

A few months later I was happy to learn that she had donated most of her inheritance to a children's home and was devoting her spare time to handicapped youngsters. She had found a new purpose in life. She was looking youthful and cheerful again. She had received infinitely more than she had given.

Once again it was another person who had opened my eyes to a basic truth. It was now quite obvious to me that happiness and a passion for life are forces that irradiate the whole human being and find expression in a more youthful appearance. The young look young both because of their bodily youth and internal youth — that is, their enthusiasm for and belief in life. We have only a limited power over the age of our body, but we have almost absolute command over our belief in life. Retaining one's enthusiasm and passion for life permits us to salvage at least that part of our youth. My memory reviewed briefly some of the happiest people I had known in my life and, true enough, none of them, despite their age, gave me the impression of being old. The youth and exuberance of their mind and heart had counterbalanced the physical toll of time. Who, for example, in the

United Nations would have ever considered Benjamin Cohen, Paul Hoffman, U Thant, or Raul Prebisch to be old men?

Since then, whenever I meet an elderly person who looks young, I ask: "Is it happiness that makes you look so youthful?" The answer is usually affirmative, sometimes with a slight hesitation, as if people were ashamed to acknowledge their bliss.

I thus learned that happiness is not only a factor of serenity but also a very potent recipe for youth. I only wish that some medical research were devoted to the effects of happiness on health, healing, youth, beauty, and longevity.

VOLUME THREE
Lessons from Nature

Grethel and My First Cherry Tree

There is incomparable happiness in the love for nature and for animals. We must give this joy to all children,

Two of the earliest memories in my life concern a black hen and a cherry tree.

The hen's name was Grethel. I owned her for about a year after my parents moved from Belgium back to Alsace-Lorraine. My father could not find a job as a hatmaker and worked as a glazier in the chinaware factory of Sarreguemines. He was entitled to share a small house with a fellow worker named Gabriel, a fireman in his spare time for whom I had great admiration because he wore a beautiful uniform and a shiny brass helmet when going to church on Sundays. The house had a garden, at the end of which stood a chicken coop. There lived Grethel, my black hen, my great love at that time. I do not know how she managed to understand her name and to respond to it, but the truth is that when I called her she flew from the end of the garden straight into my arms.

I was four years old. This was the age when images of the first snow, of hungry birds feeding on the windowsill, of drops of rain gliding along electrical lines, of swallows in the summer sky, and of pussy willows in the spring engrave themselves deeply on a child's memory. There was so much to see, so much to wonder about, so much joy in observing the world. I could stay for hours behind the kitchen window and watch the birth and death of snowflakes or the movements of a hungry finch. I could contemplate endlessly the play of the sun rays in my room or the limpid waters of a brook meandering among the tender grasses and flowers of spring.

After a year or so, my father decided to enter a business venture: He borrowed money and bought a set of hatmaking machines from a firm that had gone out of business in Saarbrücken, the capital of the neighboring Saar Territory. He installed the equipment in an attic and opened shop in the Goldstrasse, the alley of the Jews, a side street on the outskirts of the main business center of our hometown.

There were no gardens in that neighborhood, and I had to part with Grethel. My father decided to give her away to a farmer, and I was allowed to take her there myself. I have never forgotten those sad moments. It was evening and raining. My mother was accompanying me. I wore a little hooded raincoat, with black-and-white dots, under which I kept Grethel tightly in my arms, protecting her from the rain and giving her all my warmth and love. I was crying silently, kissing her little head and beak, and talking softly to her all the way. My heart was bursting with pain. I was the unhappiest little boy on planet Earth, and I thought that I would not survive my sorrow. But it was just the first experience of a permanent separation in life.

My father saw that severance from nature would render his children very unhappy. Therefore, the following June, he took us to an orchard and showed us a magnificent cherry tree, loaded with dark red, glaring juicy fruits. It was a middle-aged tree at the height of its production. My father said to us:

"This cherry tree is yours. I bought its entire crop. You can come here as often as you want and pick the fruits."

I have never forgotten the joy that that tree gave us. After Grethel, it was definitely one of the greatest events of my early childhood. Ever since, cherries have represented to my eyes a kind of sacred, joyful fruit especially created by the gods for little boys and girls. Whenever later during my life I saw a child eat cherries, I stopped to contemplate the scene with deep gratification.

My dream was of course to have my own cherry tree some day. That dream came true many years later in a place I would have never expected: the United States. In 1968, I was transferred from the UN in Geneva, Switzerland, to New York. My wife and I made a special trip to America before moving with the entire family. We wanted absolutely to find a house in Dobbs Ferry, a charming little village in the Hudson Valley, where we lived previously and where three of our children were born. After a few days of fruitless search, we were about to abandon hope when we were offered a small house tucked between big mansions near the Ardsley golf course. We visited it on a rainy and gray Sunday, under the worst possible conditions to buy a house. My wife was inspecting the inside, while I was wandering through the garden, protecting myself from the downpour with an umbrella. The grounds were very spacious and consisted of a lawn, a vegetable garden, flower beds, and an orchard. In the latter, two venerable cherry trees were bearing loads of fruit! My heart rejoiced. It was very rare to find fruit trees in the suburbs of New York, but the doctor who owned the house loved gardening and he had even grown a little vineyard from which he made his own wine! This house had to be ours. My wife had reached the same conclusion. We looked at each other very excitedly and went to church, praying that God would help us gather the money needed for the purchase. Here we would be happy, very happy indeed, and I would not be homesick for my beloved Europe. God must have heard us, for we were able to meet the conditions of the owner, and in the afternoon we signed the first papers leading us to ownership. Nobody would henceforth be able to take this jewel from us.

Since then I have planted many fruit trees on our land. In all seasons they have given me great happiness. Seldom a day passes when I do not pay them a visit, talk to them, touch them, care for them, and watch them grow. There is so much joy in a fruit tree, from its beautiful flowers in spring to that sacred, incomparable moment of picking the first ripe fruits in fall. I am not at all surprised that a golden apple was made the symbol of temptation in Paradise!

I only wish that more people would again plant fruit trees and give this joy to their children. I have advocated it often in my speeches on the environment. Perhaps the world would be a better place if people were seeking again the simple happiness of their backyards instead of rushing to faraway countries, anonymous fortunes, and senseless power. Voltaire was so right when he concluded his *Candide* with a simple and wise precept: *Cultivez votre jardin* (Tend to your garden).

Strangely enough, fate provided me with an opportunity to do something for fruit trees in my hometown. In January 1974, on the occasion of a trip to Europe with Secretary General Waldheim, I was received by the Town Council of Sarreguemines. The mayor, Robert Pax, a former schoolfriend of mine, invited me for dinner the evening before the reception, and we reminisced about the past. We particularly thanked God for having graced us with survival, since so many of our playmates had been killed during the war in French or German uniforms. The losses had been so terrible that after the war it was painful for us to walk in the streets and to meet the eyes of our dead friends' mothers in which we could read only one question: Why is he alive and not my son?

I asked the mayor:

"Where are the fruit trees of our youth? I barely see any left. How can the children of this town be happy if they ignore the pleasure of trees flowering in spring and maturing in fall? Do you remember how each year we knew exactly which trees would ripen first and how thrilled we were to taste the first apples or pears? Do you recall how we loved to accompany the mayor and the municipal councilors when they auctioned off rows of trees along public roads?"

He remembered it very well but confessed that all this had gone. People nowadays did not even bother to pick the fruits hanging on the last trees in their gardens. Apples, pears, grapes, cherries, and plums came from places as far away as California, South Africa, Israel, and Chile. He could foresee the day when there would be no fruit trees left at all in the region.

"This is precisely what is wrong with our world," I said. "We rely too much on what people produce for us in faraway countries, sometimes located on the other side of the globe. Why should a salad, a tomato, or an apple have traveled and consumed energy over thousands of miles before reaching our tables? Could they not be grown in our backyards? Would they not taste better? Someday we will wake up with great pain when some of these supplies will be cut off for one reason or another. Remember the wisdom of Voltaire and of our forefathers. The world has become too interdependent, too fragile. When I was born in 1923 there were 11 cities in the world with a population of more than 1 million inhabitants. Today there are 160, and by the year 2000 there will be more than 300. Who will guarantee the supply of adequate food, energy, water, and fresh air to all these giant agglomerations? Can you imagine the problems this will pose for humanity — the peace, understanding, and co-operation it will require from all nations?"

The following day, at the meeting at City Hall, we exchanged views on the state of the world and of our town, only to discover that the problems were the same: a growing population, industrialization, pollution, water shortages, the retreat of nature, youth unrest, and so on and so forth. I thought that I was sitting in a United Nations meeting in New York! The mayor referred to the conversation we had had the day before and said to his Council:

"Our friend from overseas is right. We have neglected our heritage of fruit trees to the point of near extinction. We must do something about it and give again to our children the joy and lessons of the blooming, ripening, and harvesting of fruit trees. I propose that we return to the tradition of our forefathers and plant again fruit trees along our public roads, in our parks, and on our municipal land."

I closed my eyes surreptitiously for a fraction of a second and saw in my heart the images of Grethel, of my first cherry tree, and of my kind father, the hatmaker, who had taught me to deeply love God's nature and living creatures. His lesson had not been in vain. He had taken the pains of revealing to us the deep joy there is in the fruits of the earth and in all living beings. Ever since, nature has been for me a source of bliss, an endless book of study and observation, and one of the surest ways of perceiving the great mysteries of creation and life. Wherever I am and whatever I do, my heart always longs for nature. There is not a spell of sadness, despair, or doubt that the contemplation of nature and of its miraculous fruits does not help me to heal.

Lessons from My Elders

The Last Palm Leaf

Love for one's profession can be one of the greatest sources of happiness.

If I have ever known two people who lived happy lives, they were my father and my grandfather. Their example has guided me throughout my life. Many times, when I feel discouraged, a simple image comes back to my mind, restoring forthwith my faith and confidence: the sight of my father, joining us in the kitchen at mealtimes and showing us with a glowing and happy face a new hat he had made. He stood in front of us, dressed in an overall white blouse, slowly twirling the hat on the tip of his fingers and waiting for our praise. Such a smiling and joyful face one can rarely see today. His eyes in particular reflected his inner happiness. No narcotics on earth could ever achieve a similar glow.

Often he climbed from his workshop in the basement to my room, located on the highest floor of the house, where I was studying, and I heard the heavy thumps of his wooden shoes on the steps of the long staircase. I knew that he was coming to show me another of his masterpieces. Once he said to me, and I have never forgotten his words:

"Son, I have the most beautiful profession on earth. I would not exchange it for any other work in this world. I hope that all my life I will be able to make hats."

How many times have I repeated the same words:

"I have the most beautiful profession on earth. I would not exchange it for any other work in this world. I hope that all my life I will be able to labor for peace."

To be happy, my father did not have to see his business grow by 8 per cent a year or by any other percentage, as is the case today of so many enterprises. Together with another hatmaker, he served his town and was content to make an average of forty to fifty hats a week during the peak seasons, in spring and in the fall. The same was true of my uncle the baker, my uncle the butcher, and of most artisans of our town.

I have similar fond recollections of my grandfather.

It seems difficult to believe that at one time Panama hats were manufactured in Alsace-Lorraine! My grandfather was one of the main producers, and many memories of that time remain vividly engraved in my memory. I loved to spend vacations at his house and factory, and there was not a detail of production that escaped my attention. I was fascinated by the strange large palm leaves coming from faraway, exotic lands, which were transformed into beautiful, white, flexible straw hats.

The industry started in the 1880s, after Alsace-Lorraine became German and when Germany acquired large overseas colonies. Several industries for processing colonial raw materials were established in our region. Panama hats were produced in South America. They were reputed for their beauty, flexibility, and durability, but not many of them entered international trade, since they were handwoven in very limited quantities by Indians in Ecuador.[1] They were extremely fashionable and in great demand at that time. Germany therefore decided to import leaves of the Carloludovica palm and to have the hats manufactured in its poorer regions, such as the Black Forest and Crooked Alsace, an area straddling the borders of Alsace and Lorraine. There labor costs were low, and manufacturing (that is, hand-made) was an adjunct to agriculture.

Copying the Indians of the Altiplano, my grandfather's workers dipped long rows of leaves hanging from poles into big kettles of boiling water. The large steaming room where these kettles were located

---

[1]They were known as Panama hats because sailors bought them in Panama.

was called the *Kesselhaus*. Then the leaves were spread into the open air for bleaching and thereafter hung again on long movable poles and placed for several days in small barracks (*Schwefelkasten*) where sulphur was burned to render the straw mold-resistant under the wet climates of Europe. The leaves were then taken to factory rooms called *Spaltenzimmer* (*spalten*: splitting), where workers pulled them through rows of equidistant razor blades in order to obtain a bundle of regular straw strips ready to be handwoven into hats. Horse-driven wagons and a couple of drivers delivered loads of these strips to the peasants who, during the long winter months, earned an additional income weaving hats. These were regularly collected and after pressing and finishing, were shipped all over Europe.

Mountains of dried palm leaves were kept in the enormous attic of the house and in a vast barrack especially built for their storage. Summer and winter, my sister and I had great fun in gliding down the slopes of these mounds, and I have often thought that it should be possible to ski and sleigh on slopes of dried palm leaves in arid regions of the world.

The factory was located in Sarralbe, on the banks of the River Sarre. It was bustling with people when I was a child. It had a delightful, pleasing odor of dried, sunny Panama leaves. *Schreibers* (clerks), installed behind high, slanted wooden desks, were billing the merchandise, writing by hand business letters and keeping records and accounts in enormous ledgers. My tall, proud grandfather was supervising all operations, walking through the factory, dressed in an immaculate white overall blouse, his Kaiser Wilhelm mustache carefuly curled and elegantly protruding. Hearty meals were prepared by women in an enormous kitchen on the first floor, from which one had direct access to the attic filled with palm leaves. As a little boy, I was constantly running from the one to the other. In the living room, or *Gute Stube* (the Good Room), three objects always retained my attention: an oil painting of my great-grandfather, also a hatmaker; a silver sword that my grandfather proudly wore on Sundays when going to church; and a magnificent German encyclopedia from the year 1894, which contained the most beautiful plates and drawings a little boy could dream of. In later years my grandfather gave me the volumes one by one until they were all in my possession. They fortunately survived the war and are still one of my most cherished belongings.

In the 1930s the European straw hat industry began to decline, mainly as a result of competition from Japan, where straw hats and even sturdy substitute paper hats were being produced at unbeatable prices. One factory in Sarre-Union survived up to the present day by switching to felt-hat production. My grandfather decided instead to progressively retire until all activity had subsided, and the factory died its natural death. But he continued to own it and to love it dearly. Each time I visited him, he showed it to me with great pride, room by room, reminiscing about the beautiful past. Knowing the premises by heart, I was much more fascinated in watching his reactions, his face, and the expression of his tremendous inner feelings. He too had loved his profession immensely, and one of his greatest joys was that my father, his second son, had also become a hatmaker.

I was fully trained as a hatmaker too, both in felt and in straw, and my hatmaker's certificate has always been a cause of great pride for me. But above all, my father's and my grandfather's happiness in their profession never ceased to be a source of inspiration and emulation for me.

One day, I was accompanying a newly appointed Secretary General to Africa, where we visited several countries, made many speeches, and worked very hard. In the evening, as we were relaxing and chatting, he asked me:

"How do you do it? How do you manage to know so much about the world, its peoples, their aspirations, their soul, and their needs?"

I answered:

"It is very simple. All you have to do is to deeply love your profession." And I told him the story of my proud father and grandfather, concluding:

"At the United Nations it is not very different. Our duty is to love our work for mankind. The world is our material, as felt and straw are the materials of a hatmaker. We must know it inside and out, its composition, its qualities and its defects, its strength and its points of weakness, its beauties and its blemishes. The people are our customers and we must serve them well. We must therefore think of the world and the people at all times. We must wake up in the morning and go to rest in the evening with the world and its people in our hearts and on our minds. One day you will wake up and think of Africa and its people. The right thoughts will come to you. They will never leave you and will stand ready at your service at the opportune moment because they were deeply felt and consequently right."

1939: Sarralbe was evacuated when the war broke out. My grandfather left the town and managed as a refugee without any help from his children.

1940: The little town was terribly devastated. Two bombs hit the living quarters of the factory. Most of my grandfather's belongings were destroyed.

1940 to 1945: With great courage my grandfather undertook the repair and reconstruction of the property.

1946: After the job was done, he invited his five children and all his grandchildren to a big family reunion in his home. He was now over eighty years old. He made a very moving speech in which he revealed that all his labors during the past few years had one sole objective: to see once again all his kin gathered around him in his rebuilt home. It was a very moving reunion indeed. If only someone could have recorded what went on in all our minds and hearts during those precious, reminiscing moments when the whole family felt like one living body.

A week later we were called again to his house to pay him our last respects: His goal having been attained, the nerves of life abandoned him, and he died peacefully of old age with one of his daughters and myself holding vigil at his side.

Every time I return to Alsace-Lorraine, I pay a visit to my hometown and to my grandfather's tomb in Sarralbe. In 1973, I had another such occasion: Secretary General Waldheim had asked me to accompany him to Geneva, where he presided over a meeting of the heads of all United Nations agencies and also negotiated with the Foreign Minister of South Africa, Mr. Hildegard Muller, for the independence of Namibia, the former German Südwestafrika, where most of the palm leaves of my grandfather had come from! Before returning to New York, the Secretary General decided to spend a day or two in Salzburg to keep in touch with his country and people. I decided to do the same and made a quick trip to Sarralbe. There, the factory of my grandfather had been sold to the municipality, which used it as a shelter for its fire engine and as a workshop for a locksmith. The grounds had also been sold and on the site there now stood a supermarket.

For several years I had not set foot in the old building where in all likelihood there was nothing to see. But this time I said to one of my uncles: "Let us go and visit grandfather's old place and see what has become of it."

The grounds were appalling and typical of the new world we live in: empty plastic bottles and all kinds of refuse scattered between the supermarket and the Sarre River, old scraps and machinery stacked up and rusting in ugly heaps in the open air, the beautiful river in which I had had such pleasure swimming in, all polluted, green, filthy, and soapy. I almost cried at these sights and at the remembrance of the beautiful place it was when, each Easter, as a little boy, I ran all over the grounds to hunt for the Easter eggs that my grandfather had hidden behind the bushes or in the tall grass. It was hard to believe that I had been such a happy, dreamy boy on that riverbank, observing each flower and insect, knowing exactly how far my feet could go into the reeds until they reached the water. I looked around and saw no little boys on the grounds. Did they avoid them because of the filth and the plastic bottles? No. In all likelihood they were watching television!

I turned my eyes away from these sad dumping grounds and said to my uncle:

"Let us go inside the house."

"You cannot do that. The place no longer belongs to us."

Nevertheless, I went ahead. The front door was open. The wooden floor was still the same. I remembered how the rays of the sun used to move over it, highlighting the rough fiber of the overwashed wood. Deep in the corridor I recognized the iron railing of the staircase leading to the first floor. The details of its forgings were engraved in my memory. I could have guessed which step of the staircase was going to squeak under my feet. I said to my uncle:

"Here, near the staircase, you used to keep your old-fashioned one-wheel cycles, and there on the right side was the *Kesslerei*. Somewhere around here also was a wooden trap leading to the cellars."

Indeed it was still there. Unfortunately it was locked, as were the doors to the former offices and to the apartments. But I did not abandon my efforts. At the other end of the long building I heard the sound of a hammer on an anvil. I opened the door. A lonely elderly man was working in a locksmith shop. My uncle presented me to him as his nephew from America. My eyes were eagerly scanning the place:

"This was the *Färberei*, a very dark place of steaming kettles filled with different colors. This wooden staircase leads to the attic. Let us go up there."

"*Du bisch verrickt*" (You are crazy), said my uncle in Lorraine dialect. "I have not been up there since your grandfather died."

But I went ahead and he followed me reluctantly.

We found ourselves in the vast old attic, practically unchanged, for the bombs had not hit that part of the building. I recognized the roof, the old beams, the stone walls, and a ladder that still hung there. One corner of the attic was occupied by a little playroom made of wooden partitions. My uncle suddenly became quite excited and exclaimed:

"But this was my hideout! I cannot believe it. It has not changed since my boyhood."

And his hands were fumbling for remnants of his past and finding them. He even extracted from a wooden shelf an old poster from the 1920s.

But where there had formerly been mountains of palm leaves, the attic now contained only old discarded furniture from the local school, a real paradise of antiques. There were also a few high desks that belonged to my grandfather. My eyes were feasting on the smallest details, trying to revive the past and to catch glimpses of old images and emotions. And they became alive like little sparrows in the warmth of a hand. In the middle of the attic someone had swept together a heap of dust. Something yellow was shining in it. I bent down and pulled out . . . a palm leaf! It was cut in strips by a hand that had died long ago. It was all dusty and dirty, flappy and devoid of life after so many years. But it was a palm leaf, all right, the last of millions of palm leaves that had passed through my grandfather's factory, formerly animated with joy and life, today dead except for the sound of the hammer of an old workman. . . . I kept it preciously while my uncle was scolding me:

"You are really nuts. You cannot leave this place with that old dirty palm leaf and walk around with it in the village. What will people think of you? Take at least a piece of newspaper and wrap it up in it." And he kept repeating half admiringly:

"*Du bisch a Stick Vieh*" (You are quite a character).

I took my precious find with me to America, where I cleaned it carefully, blade by blade. Together with grandfather's encyclopedia, it is one of the rare objects left of the rich and sunny life of Panama hat-making in the village of Sarralbe in Lorraine. It reminds me what a profound source of happiness love for one's work can be.

The lives, the rich and happy lives, of my grandparents and parents have already vanished from this world and are engulfed in oblivion, except for a little corner of a heart that still beats in a tall glass skyscraper in New York City but that will also stop and pass away someday. For years a big factory had been bustling with life, giving rise to employment, joy, craftsmanship, and happiness, and today there is barely a handful of inhabitants left in the village who would remember that it ever existed. All things are transient on this earth, be it power, glory, wealth, and even entire civilizations. All we can do is to put our full love into our lives, professions, and families, making a work of art of the few precious years that are granted to us. This is the lesson my grandfather and father, the happy hatmakers, gave me when I was a boy, and I hope to leave similar dear recollections to my children.

Of Daily Blessings

Every day count one of your blessings.

One of the great regrets in my life is that I knew only one of my grandparents. In the 1920s longevity was not what it is today. My mother's parents died while she was a child, and my father's mother passed away before I was born. I knew therefore only my paternal grandfather, the hatmaker. Today I feel that my father and mother had the greatest influence on my life, but when I was a child my grandfather was my god and hero. My father was too involved in his own affairs, worries, and beliefs, and he was constantly preaching and thinking that he was right and that I was wrong. My grandfather was different: He was old, smiling, gentle, and in a constant state of love with me. He told me stories that were close to my world: the world of nature, animals, and legends. Through his stories he transmitted to me the wisdom he had acquired in his life. I knew that he was telling the truth, for at his age he had no ax to grind and no interest in telling me lies. Furthermore, he knew that my father's daily work, business, and sleepless nights were not understandable to me. He sensed that I wanted basically to know the world as a beautiful place. He knew that the world of the very young and of the very old is essentially the same, namely a world of miracles one is about to discover or to lose. We were much closer to the truth than middle-aged people.

My grandfather taught me that every day in life I should be thankful for one of my blessings:

"You will never obtain everything in life but you will always be blessed with so much. Whatever your situation is, there will always be someone more unfortunate than you. Think of him and thank God for all the good things you have. One day, remember how lucky you are to possess two eyes. There are many blind people in the world. Think of them and be grateful for the wonderful world you can see: the flowers, the animals, the sunshine, the stars, the brooks, and the meadows. How terrible you would feel without eyesight. Another day, when you eat, think of the hungry. A third day, when you play, think of the crippled. A fourth day, when you go to school, think of those who have no schools. When your mother kisses you, think of those who have no mother. When you look at my gray hair, think of the beauty of youth. And many years hence, when you will be old, think how lucky you are to be still alive, to be blessed with one more day, to be wise, and to have a little grandson like you. . . ."

He inculcated this basic belief deeply into me through innumerable wonderful children's stories, which taught me more about life than all I learned later in school.

Today, whenever despair menaces me, the image of my grandfather comes back. I hasten to count my blessings, I concentrate on one of them, and almost forthwith my worry vanishes or takes on a more reasonable proportion.

The world, alas, has lost the habit of counting its blessings. Often when I speak to audiences with optimism about humanity's future, I hear the most devastating comments on the world's condition. Then I think of the time of my youth and describe the kind of world in which I lived. It was a very poor world indeed, the Europe of that time. We ate meat only once a week, on Sunday. Our nourishment consisted of heavy soups at luncheon and of boiled potatoes, cottage cheese, and onions in the evening. Still I never saw a loaf of bread being cut without my father making the sign of the cross on it. Peasants took off their caps and crossed themselves when they passed near a field of wheat. We had only one precious pair of shoes, and the purchase of new ones for our growing feet was an object of long discussion in the family. I saw workers walk with their shoes tied around the neck in order to spare them. The weakest electric bulbs were used to save on electricity when that form of light replaced the gas lamps. My eyesight suffered and I lived the yearly ordeal of needing costly, new, stronger glasses. I often heard my parents speak of women who had died in *Kindbett* (in childbirth; literally, "in child's bed"). I could

not understand what it meant to die in a child's bed. Only later did I
learn that many mothers died at the moment of giving birth. There
was so much misery all around. On Saturday evenings, I could hear
screams of women being beaten by their drunken husbands who out
of misery had squandered their paycheck in a pub to seek a moment
of well-being. And still, it was a beautiful life, a wonderful world, for
there was always a wise old man or woman to listen to, a bird to be
watched, an insect to be observed, a morning Mass to be attended, a
royal meal to be expected at Christmas and Easter, those two high
points of the year. And what a miracle it was to receive the first toy or
chocolate or to see the first oranges and bananas appear in the mar-
ket. Yes, things that we take for granted today, such as food, were considered absolutely sacred. We were never allowed to leave any food on
our plates. If we didn't like a meal, it was warmed up time and again
for days until we ate it. All this is gone today in our affluent world.
People are seldom grateful for what they have and usually want endlessly more. What pains I had to teach my children to cut useless
lights in the house or to stop the faucets a little earlier. They could not
understand why it upset me so when they left the tiniest grain of rice
on their plate, until one day I had them calculate how many tons and
shiploads of rice it represented each year if 4 billion people wasted a
grain three times a day. The same is true for a drop of water, for a watt
of electricity, or for a sheet of paper. As long as people will not be able
to think in these terms, all the crises of Western civilization — be it
the environment, food, energy, water, or inflation — will never be
resolved. No governmental decree will suffice. Only the will of
restraint of the 4 billion inhabitants of planet Earth will do the job. I
wonder what my grandfather would have said if he had learned that
it would take 56 million gallons of water, 37,000 gallons of gasoline,
5 1/2 tons of meat, 9 tons of milk and cream, 48 tons of steel, etc., to
sustain an American over an average lifetime! He would have
answered that such a life was tempting God and that it would end in
world catastrophe. Well, he would not have been too far from the
truth, to judge from the recent global crises. He would have been
appalled by the lack of gratefulness amid our abundance. He would
have recommended also that we give back to the children their grand-

parents, that we keep them in the warmth of our families so that they may teach the wisdom of life to the young, a wisdom they no longer get from parents, schools, political leaders, and the media. He would have requested that the old people's homes be closed and that the elderly be begged to come back and perform again their most precious and inalienable function: the transmission of wisdom in the eternal chain of life that links generation to generation on our beautiful but forever incomprehensible journey in the universe.

Abbé Pierre

*We need to be needed. Service to others can give us a new
purpose in life.*

One has sometimes the good fortune of meeting in life one of those
rare human beings who are able to convey to their fellow men in a
very short time a forceful and unforgettable message about a basic
human truth. Among such persons I will never forget the French
priest Abbé Pierre. I met him shortly after the war in Geneva,
Switzerland, where I was attending meetings of the United Nations.
We had as neighbors the family of a Hungarian UN staff member,
Lazslo Hamori, a man with a great heart and a boundless gentleness,
whose life was devoted to youth organizations and humanitarian
causes. Lazslo Hamori is dead today, but his inspired, generous smile
and his expression of inner happiness still stir in me moving memories. During our stay in Geneva he once said to me:

"I am sure you would be pleased to meet a friend of mine and a
great man for whom I have a deep affection and admiration, Abbé
Pierre. He is coming to Geneva to officiate at the wedding of the
daughter of a garbage collector who is a member of his organization
called the "Disciples of Emmaus."

I gladly accepted and so, one evening, we had dinner at the
Hamoris' where we met a sturdy, broad-shouldered, bearded man
dressed in rough priestly cloth and wearing enormous, thick-soled
worker's shoes. His total appearance was a mixture of strength and
suffering, of torment and peace. He spoke sparingly during the dinner, but at coffee time, when Lazslo Hamori asked him to narrate his
life, he suddenly seemed to leave us for another world.

From his heavy mass of flesh and bones came a flow of soft, inspired words, the feelings and depth of which only a great writer could render truthfully. To the best of my recollection, this is what he said:

"It was shortly after the war. I had been severely ill for a long time and I was despairing of heaven and earth. Nothing seemed to make sense any more. My sickness, the horrors of the war, the hatred and the misery of the people had broken my courage. There was no hope, no determination left in me. I was a floating wreck on the stream of daily events. My parish was located in one of the poorest Parisian suburbs, a workers' community where I could see only misery and despair. One day the police called me to the bedside of a poor fellow in a shabby hotel. The man had attempted to commit suicide by cutting his wrist. He was a former criminal who had just been released from the French penitentiary of Cayenne in French Guiana. I did my best to comfort him, but my own state of despair was such that I could not find the proper words of consolation and hope for him. I merely said:

"'My poor fellow, how am I expected to help you when I am in such desperate need of help myself?'

"Strangely enough, these words seemed to enliven his eyes in which I caught a flicker of interrogation and interest. "He answered:

"'Father, do you mean to say that there might be on this earth someone more miserable than I, someone who might need my help?'

"His words were a revelation to me. They aroused me from my lethargy. His message was that man's greatest need was to be needed by others, to be of service to others. I hastened to confide in him my personal miseries. In return, he confessed to me that he had wanted to die because there was no one left on earth who cared for him.

"While he spoke, I could suddenly visualize the multitude of poor fellows like him who were craving to be of help to others in the world, who wanted to be full, useful human beings and to be part of the celebration of life. Nobody, I thought to myself, should ever be allowed to fall as low as not to be needed by someone else. What could society do for such people? What could I do for them?

An idea suddenly arose in my mind: Why not get together with other shipwrecks like him and do something for people still poorer and more miserable than ourselves?

"Hope and joy came back to my life when we both founded the Disciples of Emmaus, an association of outcasts, desperados, and former criminals. First in Paris and later in other cities of France and Europe, people like us gathered and collected garbage, rummage, and refuse, sold whatever was salable, and from the proceeds helped the poor. This cause gave us a new purpose in life, and with it came health, happiness, and faith."

Abbé Pierre became dreamier and dreamier as he went on speaking. He was no longer with us. He spoke about the world and the need of people everywhere, especially the young, to be of service to others.

"The fathers have built cathedrals and there is nothing left for their sons to do except to be caretakers. . . . We must give youth new challenges, new dreams, new cathedrals to erect. . . . Poverty is still an immense frontier on this planet. . . . We must help the young to be of help to others and to make this world a beautiful place. . . ."

Thus, many years before nations became aware of the youth problem, Abbé Pierre had had a premonition of it. He started the first peace corps, composed of young Swedes, whom he sent to work in the slums and shantytowns of Latin America. The message received at the bedside of the poor outcast in Paris inspired Abbé Pierre endlessly. Best known among his initiatives was his postwar self-help building program: He obtained from the French Government free sites and small-scale equipment — such as concrete mixers, shovels, and wheelbarrows — with which the workers, helping each other, built their own dwellings. Near practically every big town in France sprang up one of the famous "cities of Abbé Pierre."

I never met again this remarkable man, the son of a wealthy silk merchant of Lyon, who had chosen for his earthly destiny the company and the path of the poor. From time to time I receive scanty news about him through an organization called Citoyens du Monde (World Citizens), of which he is a prominent and faithful member. I never forgot this evening and his inspired words. How many times did they come back to my mind during my life!

Thus, in 1972, we were again spending the summer near Geneva, this time in our own farmhouse in St. Gix, a tiny hamlet at the foot of the Jura Mountains in France. One day, when I was visiting our carpenter in the neighboring village of Vesancy, I heard him ask his wife:

"Where is our son? I would like him to meet Mr. Muller." She answered:

"He went out with some friends to collect iron scrap in the village." And she turned to me with these words:

"We are so grateful to Abbé Pierre for having created the Disciples of Emmaus. Thanks to him our children have a purpose and keep away from mischief."

A few days later I was called away from our vacation to accompany Secretary General Waldheim on his first official visit to the People's Republic of China. In this faraway country my thoughts once again turned to Abbé Pierre when I saw an entire society, in towns and villages, organized on the principle of mutual help. Undoubtedly this accounted for the people's mysterious and unforgettable happiness in the midst of their limited material welfare. A comment came to my lips:

"To say that all this has been accomplished without belief in God! And yet, if Jesus were to return to Earth, he would probably give China one of his highest marks!"

Throughout the vagaries of history, beyond ideologies and systems, a few basic truths command the justice and happiness of men and societies. Service and kindness to each other are two of them. In our Western world, greed, accumulation, and outsmarting one another — if not sheer robbery and exploitation — have gone too far. Is it not urgent for all people and nations to rediscover the virtues of honesty, morality, self-restraint, and devotion to common causes? These virtues provide an immense fund of individual reward and satisfaction and a vast outlet for the generous aspirations of youth. They are the cornerstones of a better and a happier world.

And why should we not dethrone also in international relations the supremacy of power, interest, distrust, and subversion, by ideals of co-operation, mutual help, and understanding? Is it such an impossible dream? Whether we like it or not, it will come lest we perish. It is high time to establish compassion, love, care, and mutual help at the center of world relations as we do in our families, in our cities, and in national affairs. This is the great lesson Abbé Pierre left with me. It had an indelible effect on me for the rest of my life. I had entered the United Nations with an ideal. From that day on it became a religion, the religion of public service, of work not based on mere intelligence, knowledge, skill, and reward, but on the heart, feeling, commitment to doing good, and to being of service to others. Oh if only all public services of the world could become true religions, imbued with the deepest passion for the people's welfare and happiness! Then the world would indeed become a better place to live in.

The Advice of a General

Life must be planned as a harmonious whole. Old age must be visualized at an early stage.

Often when I ponder about the meaning of life, an old scene comes back to my memory. It was in 1953, shortly after my marriage. During our first visit to France, I wanted to introduce my young wife to prominent Frenchmen and friends who had played an important role during the war and in the underground. Among them was General Koenig, an Alsatian who had joined De Gaulle to fight the Germans in Africa and later became the commander-in-chief of the French underground forces. He was one of the most admired heroes in France, and I wanted my wife to meet this compatriot of mine from Alsace-Lorraine.

General Koenig, dressed in civilian clothes, received us in a manner so amicable and gentle that we immediately forgot that he was a military man. His warm, happy, life-impassioned personality was the anticlimax of uniforms, honors, and glory. It struck us forthwith that here was a man rendered exceptional by the quality of his inner happiness. His strongly featured face, both noble and rural, dominated by a hawk's nose and a martial mustache, was inundated with joy. His blue Alsatian eyes seemed to contain the entire sky, which he probed at times through the window with a wondrous look. The unique marriage of strength and happiness in this man left an indelible impression on us. To this day I am able at a moment's notice to switch on my memory to this extraordinary human being.

We talked about the war, the *maquis*, and the secret messages and parachuted arms we had received from his command. But suddenly, in the middle of the conversation, he looked intently at us, as if the young couple facing him had become extraordinarily important. He seemed to be pondering about our future and to see us not as we were just then — namely, young and full of hope — but as we would be in many years to come. After a while he broke his silence and said:

"Would you allow me to give you some advice? It would be this: Prepare yourself well for your old age, try to see your entire life right from now, and plan the fulfillment of one sole objective: happiness and contentment throughout your existence and especially at the end of it."

I have never forgotten his words. I have filled baskets of notes, souvenirs, correspondence, and treasured memories to live on during old age, if God permits. I can look with serenity toward retirement, for I have an image of the new life that will await me then. Thanks to the counsel of a general who was applying the concepts of military strategy to life itself, we designed our objectives right from the start so as to be able someday to look back on its totality and distill from it its very essence.

This has earned us profound contentment and peace, for every experience, good or bad, was a building block toward the edifice still to be erected at the end. Life is indeed man's most precious possession. It must be planned as a harmonious whole and managed with no less care than a bank account or a career. Our wisest conduct is to maximize it through good health, happiness, and longevity and to mold it to the particular conditions of each age. General Koenig was right: Life must be made the object of a strategy.

Many years later I saw again General Koenig's cheerful, eagle-nosed, and mustached face. I was addressing a group of American businessmen brought together at the United Nations by a program called "UN We Believe." After luncheon, when the group broke up, I shook hands with a man whose features had attracted me throughout the event. I asked him:

"Are you by any chance Alsatian? You look very much like General Pierre Koenig, the former commander of the French underground forces."

He answered:

"I am Robert Koenig, chairman of Foote Mineral Company. Pierre Koenig is my half brother."

Another little circle had closed itself in my life. A quarter of a century ago, General Pierre Koenig had advised us optimism and long-term planning for our lives, and here stood in front of me his kinsman asking me for the notes of my speech on the state of the world in which I had advocated foresight and long-term planning for the entire human family. Great truths have a strange way of surfacing in any place on earth. General Koenig's message had not been in vain.

Father de Breuvery and Teilhard

The great truths of visionaries always irradiate the fabric of society.

Father Emmanuel de Breuvery was one of the most remarkable men I have known at the United Nations. An entire book could be devoted to him but, alas, his UN friends and colleagues have so little time, pressed as they are by urgent world problems. Unlike his compatriot Teilhard de Chardin, with whom he served as a Jesuit in China and later shared quarters in New York, he did not leave any writings, except for his considerable work embodied in United Nations publications and achievements.

After his expulsion from China in 1951, Father de Breuvery joined the French delegation to the Organization for Economic Co-operation and Development in Paris and later to the Economic and Social Council of the UN. He was an economist of fine repute, well versed in matters of economic development, finance, and natural resources. He attracted the attention of the UN Department of Economic and Social Affairs, which offered him a post. He made his presence felt very rapidly and became director of the Natural Resources Division. There his deputy was a no less brilliant man, Joseph Barnea, an Israeli, with whom he formed one of the most dynamic and path-breaking teams of internationalists the United Nations has ever known. If the human story of this most unusual collaboration could be written, it would show what two men of totally diverse origins and beliefs can achieve when they are bound by a common concern for the fate of mankind and of our planet.

As a special assistant to the Under-Secretary General for Economic and Social Affairs, I had frequent dealings with Father de

Breuvery. We became close friends. He baptized two of our children and later, when he retired, he prompted me to return from Geneva to New York to become associate director of his division, at the helm of which Barnea had succeeded him.

Father de Breuvery often invited me for luncheon at one of his favorite restaurants: the Toque Blanche, the Cheval Blanc, or Ferdi's, just across the street from the UN. Then, after his customary man-hattan cocktail, he would talk to me about the world, its people, its resources, and the future. The tall, wiry aristocrat, who could have been a great political leader or a very successful businessman, had for the United Nations the same love and devotion he had for his Church. The UN was his family and the fulfillment of his dreams. His colleagues were his friends and teammates. Very few international civil servants did as much as he to advance some of the greatest causes of our time, such as a new order for the seas and oceans; an inventory of the world's water, energy, and mineral resources; explo-ration in the poorer countries; development of international river basins; and so on and so forth. Who remembers today that as early as 1957 he foresaw the energy crisis and convened the first UN confer-ence on new sources of energy, in Rome in 1961? Five big volumes on solar, geothermal, wind, and sea energy were then published by the UN and later reproduced in technical journals of various countries when the energy crisis broke out.

After discussing planetary issues for a while, Father de Breuvery would return to earth and test me on some of his more immediate plans and ideas.

"Muller," he said to me one day, "the post of deputy executive sec-retary of the UN Economic Commission for Asia and the Far East is vacant and has been offered to me. I am deeply tempted to accept it and resume work in Asia, where there is so much to do. But one thing troubles me: I have built up the UN Natural Resources Division and I would hate to leave it just like that. I know a young Jesuit in France who is a great expert in natural resources. I would like to see him join the division if I leave for Asia. What do you think? I know Hammarskjöld well from the days when we were both delegates to the OECD in, Paris. I am tempted to ask him for an appointment and tell him that I would accept the Asian position if my young Jesuit friend can be recruited."

Knowing perfectly well that he would do it in any case, I answered: "You do not risk anything. All Hammarskjöld can do is turn you down, and your options will still be open."

"You are right. I must try my best. As for the outcome, it lies entirely with God. He is the master, I am only his earthly servant."

Two days later he asked me again to luncheon and reported to me the outcome:

"Before entering Hammarskjöld's office I crossed myself and reminded God that it was essentially his affair. The Secretary General received me with great friendliness. We discussed a few current international issues and then I broached the question I had come to ask.

"Mr. Secretary General, as a priest I find almost complete harmony between the aims of the United Nations and those of my religion: peace, justice, progress, racial equality, nonviolence, a worldwide brotherhood for the advancement of all peoples." After these preliminaries, I was about to present my plea when Hammarskjöld interrupted me and said:

"Father, how right you are! I could not agree with you more. As a matter of fact, if you should accept the position that is offered to you in Asia, I am thinking of a Buddhist to replace you here at headquarters. . . ."

"That was obviously the end of my *démarche!* He had perfectly guessed the reason of my visit and seemed to enjoy himself tremendously! He elaborated on his offer and I politely asked for a period of reflection. Of course, I will remain at headquarters, for I cannot lose face."

Hammarskjöld did not know that his wish would come true, but in a very different way. In the same office where he spoke, at his own desk, in the same chair where he sat, amid the same furniture he had selected and ordered from Sweden, *he* was going to be succeeded, after his dramatic death, by a Buddhist and probably the most religious Secretary General the United Nations has ever known: U Thant. Perhaps God was indeed present at the meeting between the two men and was smiling at their self-assurance and ignorance of their fate.

He may have also been present when later in the same office I sat so often with U Thant, whose aide I had become, discussing the world and its peoples, while being both so utterly ignorant of our own destiny. Dag Hammarskjöld, Father de Breuvery, and U Thant are dead today, and I find myself alone with my thoughts and sentiments, trying to preserve a little echo of the past and of its cherished memories.

Father de Breuvery was a great, dynamic, and skilled man, but I was sometimes perplexed that his mind could reach so far into the future. To study and assess the world's resources was of course his job, but nobody at the UN and in government at that time was thinking more than a few years ahead. Futurology and the extension of the time horizon of man came only later. How was it then possible that an eminently practical, down-to-earth man could have foreseen the energy crisis and launched an international study program on new sources of energy as early as 1957? The thought often crosses my mind that Father Teilhard de Chardin may have influenced him. They shared an apartment in Manhattan, they confessed to each other, said Mass together, and saw each other every day. Father de Breuvery often discussed with Teilhard his work at the UN. Father de Breuvery once quoted to me Teilhard as saying:

"*Mon Père*, someday people will understand that the sun, and only the sun, from which most other forms of energy are derived, is our great clean source of energy. Among the civilizations in the universe, the earth is a very primitive one, since it uses the energy of its own planet. Others utilize the energy of their sun, and still others harness the energy of the cosmos. You must take a very long-term view, a view of hundreds of thousands of years, and prepare the minds of the political leaders to think in terms of solar energy. . . ."

On another occasion, Father de Breuvery told me:

"Last night I exploded in front of Teilhard against the UN bureaucracy. He looked at me with his kind eyes and said: '*Mon Père*, you must be patient. Mankind is still very young. Give it another five hundred thousand years and the problem of bureaucracy will also be solved!"

Such remarks often made me wonder by what mysterious ways the visions and perceptions of exceptional human beings irradiate the fabric of society. Teilhard de Chardin influenced his companion, who inspired his colleagues, who started a rich process of global and long-term thinking in the UN, which affected many nations and people throughout the world. I have myself been deeply influenced by Teilhard, although I have never been able fully to assimilate his tough, philosophical writings.

Years later, when Ellen and Mary Lukas, the authors of Teilhard's biography,[1] interviewed me on the relations between Teilhard and Father de Breuvery, they hinted to me that my own views on mankind's future were to a large extent a reflection of Teilhard's theory of convergence and fulfillment of the human race. There is, however, one difference: I firmly believe that the process will take less than a hundred years and will not require the thousands of years forecast by Teilhard. Father de Breuvery, the eminent man of action and change, would certainly have agreed with me.

[1] *Teilhard: A Biography* (Garden City, N.Y.: Doubleday & Company, 1977).

The Example of a Great Ethical Statesman: U Thant

Man can learn so much by simply opening himself to others, by lowering the barriers of his self-sufficiency and infallibility.

When I worked for him, U Thant was for me not only the Secretary General of the United Nations but also a master in the art of living. Until 1970, when I joined his staff, I did not know him very well, except for brief encounters when I served as political adviser to the United Nations troops in Cyprus. Even when I became one of his direct collaborators, I had difficulty in understanding the inner motivations of this humble and unobtrusive man. His oriental phlegm was at first a barrier to me and it took some time until I discovered that his kindness and restraint were part of a deep philosophy of life and the result of intensive training. I never heard him speak ill of another person. Considering the problems and exposures of a Secretary General, such restraint was tantamount to sanctity. I never heard him complain. Nor did I ever see him impatient or irritated. His capacity to endure the shortcomings and errors of other people was boundless. At nine or ten o'clock in the evening, after seeing dozens of visitors at quarter-of-an-hour intervals and after being bombarded by a succession of insistent problems, he was as calm and controlled as when he arrived in the office in the morning. Kindness, love, and understanding for his fellow humans were his sole motivations. Discipline and self-control were his ways.

I had to discover the richness of his person by myself, for he would have never spoken about it, so great were his humility and his respect for the other person. Two paths led me close to him: his gentle teachings and his faith.

Often, in the evening, when I presented him with a problem on which he was asked to make a decision, he simply remained silent. This was especially the case when difficulties arose between two heads of departments at the United Nations. Their memoranda requesting resolution often remained unanswered. U Thant was looking at me patiently with his kind eyes, hoping that I would understand his philosophy. And I finally did when one day I found myself holding the following language to two high officials, each of whom was looking to the Secretary General for total support:

"Can't you understand that U Thant will simply not make a decision in favor of either one of you? Your memoranda will be returned to you unanswered, no matter how often you raise the issue with him, unless you yourself take the initiative in proposing a common course of action. He feels that you know the answer to your problem much better than he does. You are well-trained and highly skilled officials. You are expected to solve problems, not to create them. The UN is preaching understanding and accommodation among nations. This is the least that can be expected from its officers. U Thant wishes you to understand that the solution rests between the two of you."

To my great surprise, the two officials agreed to a mutual solution within minutes. Both had thought of a common course, but it was to be tried only if neither could score a full victory over the other! When I reported the outcome to U Thant, he looked at me kindly and said nothing, as if he expected all people and nations to behave that way. I was beginning to grasp one of his basic beliefs namely, that truthfulness and understanding are two of the most important pillars of a peaceful and orderly society. I had learned a lesson from him which went considerably beyond the specific case and which was applicable to most human, political, and social relations.

But it was spirituality that brought me closest to the beautiful soul of U Thant. I had learned of the importance of religion in his life through the book *U Thant, the Search for Peace*[1] by June Bingham. A neighbor of U Thant, she had written his biography on the basis of interviews while she rode with him from Riverdale to mid

---

[1] New York: Alfred Knopf, 1968.

Manhattan. I made a special effort to acquaint myself with
Buddhism. After U Thant discovered that I was not the dry, prag-
matic, Western economist he first thought I was, but that I had an
inclination for humanism and spirituality, he became both a teacher
and a second father to me. He would have long conversations with me
after office hours. One evening I remember telling him that he had
made me aware again that simplicity and kindness were the highest
values a man could aim at and that he reminded me greatly of my
father, who had always taught me that love and honesty were qualities far superior to intelligence.

U Thant was really at his best when he spoke about faith and
ethics. The people he liked and admired most were religious leaders,
humanists, and great artists. His friendship with Pope Paul VI, Pablo
Casals, Norman Cousins, and Mazzone are well known. He often
invited me to luncheons and conversations with renowned visitors. I
have many cherished memories of his discussions on spirituality,
peace, and ethics with visiting humanists, Nobel Prize winners, and
other peace-loving personalities.

One day he asked me to join him in his conference room to receive
a group of Buddhists from various countries who had requested to
see him. The spokesman of the group, an articulate young American
Buddhist,[2] first gave him a general picture of Buddhism in the world
and then ended with a plea that U Thant should stay on as Secretary
General:

"We need an ethical man at the helm of the United Nations in this
troubled time. As Buddhists we are extremely happy that you occupy
this high position and we feel that it is your duty toward humanity to
stay."

I regret that I did not have a tape recorder to register U Thant's
answer, which was one of the fullest presentations of his philosophy.
He began by giving his visitors a Buddhist interpretation of the UN
Charter:

[2]I had forgotten his name, but had later the good fortune of meeting him again:
He was Ralph Buultjens, a professor at the New School for Social Research in New York.

"I have not found the slightest difficulty or contradiction between my Buddhist faith and my duties as Secretary General of the United Nations. On the contrary, in my view, the UN Charter embodies most of the essential teachings of the Lord Buddha: the principle of non-recourse to force and violence; the fostering of understanding and co-operation; the goal of harmonizing the actions of nations; and the principle of unity in diversity."

He developed these themes at length, using Buddhist terms that I am incapable of remembering. Having expounded the basic harmony between his beliefs and his duties, he commented on his daily work:

"I wake up in the morning as a Buddhist and a Burmese and meditate for at least a short while in order to set my work, actions, and thoughts into the proper perspective. When I return home in the evening, I become again a Burmese and a Buddhist: I exchange my Western clothes for the Burmese longyi[3] and reintegrate my family, which has retained fully the Burmese and Buddhist ways of life.

"But when I enter my office in Manhattan, you will understand that I must forget that I am a Burmese and a Buddhist. One of my duties is to receive many people — diplomats, political men, scientists, writers, journalists, and my UN colleagues. Most of my visitors have something specific to say to me, I must open myself to them. I must empty myself of myself. . . ."

This was Buddhism at its best. This was U Thant at his best. I have never forgotten this lesson, which has enriched my life immensely. U Thant was right: man can learn so much by simply opening himself to others, by lowering the barriers of his self sufficiency and infallibility. Relax your defenses, give access to the opinions, aspirations, knowledge, and love of others, and you will broaden yourself incredibly. After a while one becomes a crossroads, an essence of others, and consequently a more profoundly integrated member of the human society. Indeed, how can we reach full consciousness and enlightenment if we do not let the entire world and humanity enter ourselves? Humility and the lowering of one's ego lead in the end to righteousness, happiness, and the full mastery over oneself, enriched by the

---

[3] An ankle-length skirt worn by men in Burma.

thoughts, dreams, and feelings of others. Together with meditation, it is perhaps the clue to serenity in our bewildered, complex world. U Thant was a living proof of it.

At the end of the meeting with the young Buddhist and his group, the Secretary General gently but firmly reiterated his decision not to seek re-election: "A younger man is now needed in the post."

Another lesson that U Thant taught me had an even broader dimension.

The Secretary General of the United Nations receives the most fascinating mail on earth: letters from schoolchildren; from mothers; from prisoners; from people who believe that they are God and instruct him, as their son or representative on earth, to act in such or such a way; from people who threaten him, to individuals who have a plan to straighten the Pisa Tower, save Venice, pacify the Middle East, or who have declarations of independence, interdependence, liberty, equality, etc.

Among those letters one day came several long, unfolding pamphlets. A man who had worked for space programs had arranged the teachings of Buddhism in a set of tables encompassing all physical, mental, moral, and spiritual phenomena that Buddhism had identified for man on his planet and in relation to the universe.[4]

U Thant encouraged me to read the material and to discuss it with him:

"The gentleman who wrote it studied Buddhism with one of the best teachers in Burma and you will profit from reading it. I hope that someday I will be able to spend a whole weekend with you to discuss religion, ethics, and morality and tell you about my intention to write a book titled *Ethics for Our Time*, which would blend the virtues of oriental wisdom with the merits of Western dynamism."

Alas, U Thant never found the time for that project. He proceeded with my education by bits and pieces on the basis of the pamphlets, which I kept in my office. One of the tables impressed me most. It dealt with mental factors and reached from "prior birth" on the upper

[4]Robert Harry Hover, Elements of Human Interaction (Oct. 1970). Topology of Programs. P.O. Box 85, La Mirada, Calif. 90638.

left corner to "next birth and Nirvana" on the lower right side. It listed fourteen immorals — from greed, lust, and hate, to conceit, envy, and worry — and twenty-five morals — from detachment, good will, mindfulness, right speech, right action, and right livelihood, to wisdom and joy over the prosperity of others. When I showed it to U Thant, he pointed at a footnote which said:

"Closed on both ends: no prior, no next, no extrahuman life; immorals, no meditation, no prayer."

"Open both ends: belief in unlimited prior and unlimited next life; morals, prayer, Nirvana, and stream entry."

He commented: "The belief in rebirth and in immortality is very important." But as if regretting that he had spoken with a tinge of pride about his faith, he added modestly:

"To tell you the truth, I have meditated a lot in my life and I have never really reached Nirvana."

Personally, however, I felt that he had attained it and perhaps even something more: serenity, peace with himself, a kind, understanding, and loving personality. If U Thant did not reach enlightenment, I wonder if anyone ever will.

U Thant left behind innumerable friends who were touched by his inner strength and immense moral values.[5] It was not quite accurate for him to say that he divested himself of his Buddhist beliefs during his daily work. On the contrary, by practicing kindness, tolerance, serenity, and understanding, he applied his religion fully and gave a living example of the four "noble truths" set down by Buddha:

"All existence is suffering."

"Suffering is caused by desire."

"Desire can be suppressed."

"The way to suppress desire is to follow the noble eightfold path, which involves right conduct, right belief, and right meditation."

I am forever thankful to U Thant for having reminded me of the teachings of all great religions, namely that man finds bliss in seeing

[5]For testimonies of the love and respect he engendered in people, see *Meditation at the United Nations, Monthly Bulletin of the United Nations Meditation Group* (Nov. 1974), dedicated to U Thant.

himself as part of an eternal stream of life and betterment rather than as a godlike, arrogant, self-contained cluster of material interests and greed. Spirituality and righteousness were to him infinitely more important than intelligence and success.

After Trygve Lie the Robust and Hammarskjöld the Magnificent, U Thant the Kind contributed greatly, in his very unique way, to the symbiosis between world evolution and the personal qualities of the man at the helm of the world organization.

I had written most of the above text during the early-morning hours of November 25, 1974, three years after U Thant had retired from the UN. When I woke up, I had seized my notebook and without any particular reason had begun to write about U Thant. I continued to think and to write about him in the train on my way to the UN. Early in the afternoon, a UN colleague, Uner Kirdar, knocked at my office and said:

"I have very sad news for you. You have lost a good friend. I just heard over the radio that U Thant has died."

C. V. Narasimhan, the former Chef de Cabinet of U Thant and his closest collaborator for many years, was away in Tokyo, working on one of U Thant's dearest projects: the establishment of a United Nations University. After calling U Thant's family to express my grief, my first thought was to call his next closest friend, Norman Cousins. When he heard that I had been thinking of U Thant all morning and that I had written about him, he asked me for my notes, which he later published in his magazine.[6] I regret that it did not occur to me to draw his attention at that time to the following statement, which U Thant had made at a conference, "Faith and Peace," in Toronto, Canada, on October 20, 1967, written entirely in his own hand and which reflects infinitely better than my words his basic beliefs:[7]

"As is commonly known, I am a Buddhist. As a religion, Buddhism has some unique features and also some basic principles which are of

[6]"U Thant the Buddhist" (*Saturday Review*, Jan. 25, 1975).

[7]United Nations Press Release SG/SM/822 (Oct. 20, 1967). See also another remarkable statement by U Thant in Chapter Two, "How I Conceived My Role," in his book *View from the Bridge*, published by Doubleday & Company.

relevance to the theme of this teach-in. In my statement to follow I shall deal briefly with some of the cardinal principles of Buddhism which seem to me to have a direct relationship to the state of the world today.

"The doctrine taught by Gautama Buddha, which is called Dhamma, or universal principle of truth, is at once philosophy, science, ethical teaching, and the supreme way to spiritual perfection. It is all these things and more. It is different from the other religions of the world, as it has features not to be found in any of them, while at the same time it is independent of many ideas that are commonly thought to be essential to religion (for instance, the idea of a creator-God and the principle of the soul). Such concepts do not find any place in Buddhism.

"Buddhism offers to the world absolute truth: a rational explanation of the mysteries of life, of good and evil and the problem of suffering; and a way by which the ultimate reality — Nirvana — can be reached. It teaches, above all, a universal compassion, to be extended to all living beings, irrespective of their status, race, or creed. All sentient beings are involved in suffering; all are struggling in a dark ignorance that blinds them to the truth of their own nature and the laws that govern their existence. It is through the ignorance of the law of Karma that men do evil to one another, and thus to themselves. If each of us were to realize that whatsoever he does to another he does in effect to himself, through the law of reciprocal action, this world would become a happy and peaceful place. There would be no more crime, no more injustice, no more wars, and no more hatred between one nation and another. But it is in the nature of Samsara that we shall never be able to produce a perfect paradise on earth; all we can do is to mitigate the suffering wherever possible, strive to make our fellow men a little happier — no matter how bad their Karma may be — and at the same time seek to purify and ennoble ourselves. This is the only certain way to happiness, in this life and in lives to come.

"I believe that it is only in the Dhamma (the absolute truth) that we can hope to find a solution to the problems that beset us. It is only there that we can find a justification for our inherent belief in a moral order in the world — and a basis for right action, inspired by love and

compassion in our relations with our fellow men. The Dhamma
teaches us that violence will not resolve any of our conflicts. Similarly,
hatred and greed will only breed more hatred and greed.

"One of the doctrines of Buddhism has a direct relevance to pres-
ent-day conditions. It is the doctrine of selflessness or nonegoism. To
be egoistic is to be blind to the needs, and the reality, of others. In
addition, egoism is bad for oneself because it does not exist for long
by itself. It becomes, in course of time, the parent of the twin sins of
pride and prestige. If there is one lesson that history teaches us, it is
that wealth and power, pride and prestige, are not only transitory but
even illusory.

"Another doctrine of Buddhism is the universal principle of Metta
— unbounded love and compassion for all living creatures.
Buddhism teaches that the principle of nonviolence should extend
not only to other human beings but to all living things.

"I have dwelt very briefly on some important principles of
Buddhism which I believe are relevant to the human condition of
today. The universal principle of truth is obviously the most basic of
them. So many of the problems that we face today are due to, or the
result of, false attitudes — some of them have been adopted almost
unconsciously. Among these is the concept of narrow nationalism —
'my country, right or wrong.' It is lack of truth in international relations that leads to the conscious or unconscious adoption of double
standards. It is therefore essential that, in international relations as in
human relations, we should practice, as we preach to others, the universal principle of truth.

"The doctrine of Karma, the principle that every action has a reac-
tion, obviously has a direct application to international relations. The
Charter calls on us to practice tolerance and live together in peace
with one another as good neighbors. This is the practical application
of the principle of reciprocity.

"The principle of nonviolence is also a basic concept of the
Charter. One of the most fundamental principles to which member
states have committed themselves is to refrain in their international
relations from the threat or use of force. History teaches us that no
durable solution can be found for any human problem except by per-

suasion and by common consent. The use of violence is double-edged, as violence is bound by the doctrine of reciprocal action, to provoke violence in turn. Before long, we find that the rule of law has given place to the law of the jungle. We have therefore to go back to first principles and to observe the Charter commitment regarding the nonuse of violence or the threat of violence in international relations.

"The doctrine of nonegoism is equally important in international relations. Today we have in the world two superpowers, a number of major powers, and a very large number of smaller nations. It is understandable that the major powers should pursue objectives which seem to them to be in their own national interest; but they should not be blind to the existence of a larger goal, the common interest of all countries, large and small, in the survival of the human race. They should at least occasionally pause to reflect on the course of history, which has seen the rise and fall of so many great empires. Generations to come will judge the conduct of those in positions of authority today by the effect that their actions had on the course of human peace and progress. If they wish to have an honored place in human history they must appear as men of peace and not as mere victors in war.

"The law of love and compassion for all living creatures is again a doctrine to which we are all too ready to pay lip service. However, if it is to become a reality, it requires a process of education, a veritable mental renaissance. Once it has become a reality, national as well as international problems will fall into perspective and become easier to solve. Wars and conflicts, too, will then become a thing of the past, because wars begin in the minds of men, and in those minds love and compassion would have built the defenses of peace."[8]

This statement by U Thant touches upon some very fundamental principles regarding the quality of personal, social, institutional, and political life. If people and governments had a greater spirit of truthfulness and reciprocal understanding, the world would indeed become a "happy and peaceful place." Remaining conflicts would be settled rapidly. Nations would join their efforts and ascend together

---

[8]This thought has been retained for the inscription on his mausoleum in Rangoon.

toward a better world, toward Teilhard de Chardin's point of convergence. I can see U Thant's views gain ground year after year and be progressively accepted as the only realistic rules of conduct of humanity. I see the hand of fate in the fact that he was selected Secretary General of the United Nations. He was indeed a man of the future, a man of all nations and ages, a peaceful, ethical, and serene visionary of mankind's destiny. In his humble and unobtrusive way he reached the height of the greatest ethical leaders, humanists, and men of peace. He tried what seemed impossible — namely, to introduce morality and spirituality into world affairs. He was far ahead of his time, but someday scholars and historians will recognize that he was right and that his ground rules for social and political life were as momentous as Descartes' rules of thinking in the field of logic. It is appropriate in this connection to recall what U Thant said regarding his successor:[9]

"As far as the nature of the Secretary General's personality is concerned, I feel that he should be the kind of man who looks to the future, a futurist, and has a global conception of problems. I do not believe in the importance of regional considerations in the choice of a Secretary General. I do not believe that only an Asian or an African or a Latin American or a European should be the next Secretary General. What I believe in are the qualities of the head as well as of the heart, like moral integrity, competence, and his ability to project into the future, to act within the framework of a global unit, and a genuine desire to see this organization develop into a really effective instrument for peace, justice, and progress."

Such was U Thant, a great moral leader, whose presence at the helm of the United Nations was a blessing for humanity. His example will remind us for a long time that honesty, love, understanding, humility, and righteousness are the only true ways to build a peaceful, just, and happy society.

Even after his death, U Thant continued to be a teacher for me. Having read my notes published by Norman Cousins in the *Saturday Review*, U Thant's daughter Aye Aye wrote me these kind words:

[9]Press conference of January 18, 1971, United Nations document SG/SM/ 1408.

"...your article was wonderfully moving especially because Daddy cared so much that he would be remembered as a 'kind and good man who understood others' ...."

Yes, this was another posthumous lesson by U Thant: A man must care to know during his lifetime how he wants to be remembered in death. This will mold his entire life, actions, thinking, objectives, and behavior, and make him a man of righteousness and peace, a man to remember.

Knowingly or not, U Thant had applied Socrates' principle: "The nearest way to glory is to strive to be what you wish to be thought to be."

U Thant's Four Roads to Happiness

Happiness is reached through physical, mental, moral, and spiritual perfection.

Every individual sooner or later asks himself the questions: How can I lead an ideal life? How can I attain real peace and happiness? What is an optimum, fulfilled life on this planet? So many answers to those queries have been proposed over the ages — and continue to be given incessantly — that people are hardly wiser today than ever before.

Among the many recipes that were offered to me, one was particularly valuable. I owe it to U Thant. At first, I did not listen to him and found his statements on the subject somewhat bland, judged with my Western "intelligence." It was a little speech he liked to deliver to educators, students, and children — that is, people to whom one is usually anxious to leave a deeply felt message. He spoke of the body, the mind, the heart, and the spirit, and stressed the need to nourish all these four basic attributes. I often heard people comment that this was indeed a rather simple speech for a man as eminent as the Secretary General of the United Nations, but he repeated it insistently as one of his most fundamental beliefs.

During a very moving ceremony at the United Nations in December 1971, when he took leave from the UN staff in the great General Assembly hall, U Thant suddenly put aside a written speech and said the following:

> As all of you must have been aware, I have certain priorities in regard to virtues and human values. As far as I am concerned, an ideal man or an ideal woman is one who is endowed with four attributes, four qualities: physical qualities, intellectual

qualities, moral qualities, and spiritual qualities. Of course, it is very rare to find a human being who is endowed with all these qualities but, as far as priorities are concerned, I would attach greater importance to intellectual qualities over physical qualities. I would attach still greater importance to moral qualities over intellectual qualities. It is far from my intention to denigrate intellectualism or intellectual qualities but I am just trying to define my priorities. I would attach greater importance to moral qualities or moral virtues over intellectual qualities or intellectual virtues — moral qualities like love, compassion, understanding, tolerance, the philosophy of live and let live, the ability to understand the other man's point of view, which are the key to all great religions. And above all, I would attach the greatest importance to spiritual values, faith in oneself, the purity of one's inner self, which to me is the greatest virtue of all. With this approach, with this philosophy, with this concept alone, we will be able to fashion the kind of society we want, the kind of society which was envisaged by the founding fathers of the United Nations twenty-six years ago.

I have often returned to that statement and learned several lessons from it. I have come to believe that it contains indeed basic answers to many of our personal, social, national, and world problems.

I realized that, under the influence of Western education and values, my life had been directed too much to the material, scientific, and intellectual sides of life. My main concern was to "understand," to grasp with my brain, to think, to reason, and to help "rationally" build a "better" world. Perhaps this objective was moral after all, but when I looked at my life, I could not help observing that I lagged considerably behind with regard to moral and spiritual values. From the moment I included them in my objectives and gave a greater role to the heart and the soul, my life became richer, happier, and infinitely more satisfying. U Thant had simply reminded me of the basic teachings of my own Catholic faith and of the need to be guided by them during my entire life, as he was guided by his Buddhist faith.

Since then, I follow a simple practice based on U Thant's principles: Each day I try to achieve some physical, mental, moral, and spiritual improvement.

On the physical plane, it might be turning down an alcoholic drink, the avoidance of a polluting act, or an effort to do a disagreeable job particularly well. On the intellectual level, it might be the acquisition of new knowledge and wisdom, or a contribution to better world understanding. On the moral front, it might mean being kind to someone else or refraining from criticizing another person, a virtue that U Thant possessed to perfection. On the spiritual side, it might be prayer, meditation, gratitude to God, a visit to a church, contemplation of nature, or a poem in my heart. A piece of paper in my pocket serves to record what little I can accomplish and to draw there from a daily lesson.

I have often wondered what our world would be if its four billion inhabitants exerted as strenuous efforts at moral and spiritual improvement as they do nowadays on the physical and intellectual planes. What immense force it would be! What peace, justice, and love would ensue! People devote innumerable hours to material pursuits, to physical and mental satisfactions, and so little time on the heart, on the soul, on moral and spiritual joys. Sentiment, love, understanding, and compassion are considered naive and contrary to one's interests! How shortsighted this is! How far we are from a real fulfillment of man's inherited qualities, from serenity, from happiness, from just being good people with our consciences at rest. Modern man has reduced morality and spirituality to a minimum, often to a mere hour in church on Sunday. He has chased it from everyday life, from public service, political life, work, schools, and the media. How many political men and businessmen would dare to practice morality and spirituality in their offices with the same fervor as they do shrewdness and intelligence? U Thant could not understand it. And I can't either.

What applies to individuals is also valid for entire societies and for humanity as a whole. As U Thant put it: "With this approach, with this philosophy, with this concept alone, we will be able to fashion the kind of society we want, the kind of society which was envisaged by the founding fathers of the United Nations twenty-six years ago."

Our scientific and industrial age has brought incredible progress to the human race, and we should be immensely thankful for it. But this success went to our heads and led us to believe that material achievement and intelligence were the apexes of civilization. There no longer seemed to be any need for ethics, purity, morality, compassion, and love. Everything would be explained by science someday, would it not? This poverty of our age is now being increasingly recognized. The absence of truthfulness, sentiment, ethics, and humanism is the Achilles' heel of the industrial age and may be its downfall if these values are not re-established as part of a broader, richer concept of life. Multiple signs appear everywhere that material and intellectual success must now be transcended into a higher, ethical plane of life. It is a great pity that U Thant did not live long enough to give the world the *Ethics for Our Time* he intended to write. In a speech to the World Youth Forum in 1968, he said:

> One of the troubles of our times is that scientific and technological progress has been so rapid that moral and spiritual development has not been able to keep up with it. This is one of the tragedies of our time. The scientists are now exploring outer space; they are trying to get to the moon, Mars, and the stars. But we really do not know what we are going to do if we conquer outer space and get to the moon and the stars and Mars. Our moral and spiritual progress must be able to cope with the rapidly developing technology. What is necessary in these tense times is to try to develop our moral and spiritual values, in order to catch up with the technological and scientific advances.

Spiritual and moral norms were born at a time when human societies were small. They were addressed primarily to individuals. Today, we live in a world of billions of people grouped in innumerable institutions and communities. Ethical codes are therefore urgently needed for the behavior of groups and institutions. In the eyes of U Thant, the Charter of the United Nations was the first most daring code of behavior addressed to the most powerful of all institutions on this planet: armed nations. Year after year, governments now come to the United Nations and ask for new institutional codes of ethics: codes of conduct for the police and treatment of prisoners, for multinational corporations, for scientific experimentation, for international economic relations, for the behavior of governments toward the governed, of producers toward consumers, etc. A new ethical world is thus being progressively shaped in order to help humanity find a peaceful and happy life on our little planet.

We would be well advised to listen to U Thant, a man who, after ten years at the helm of the United Nations, had concluded that the greatest need of our time was to assert morality and spirituality in all human affairs, individual and collective, private and public, national and international, and that ethics and philosophy should always guide politics. The necessary knowledge, data, aspirations, and visions for a happy and just human society are now at hand. The files are almost complete. They have been derived from the painstaking efforts to probe our planetary conditions over the past thirty years, especially through a series of major world conferences. The materials for the erection of the cathedral are on the construction ground. It now remains for the leaders and for all men, women, groups, and institutions of good will to work together toward the achievement of the supreme goal: physical, intellectual, moral, and spiritual fulfillment of all peoples during their short, privileged sojourn on our beautiful planet Earth. Nothing less is worthy of the proud human race. U Thant's four categories of human qualities could become the basis for a novel worldwide ideology, a UN ideology, aimed a' guiding human life toward its optimum fulfillment.

Of Simplicity

There is nothing on earth that cannot be explained simply.

The more I live, the more I am convinced that specialization, expertise, and scientific jargon are often just a means of gaining supremacy over others. Again, in this respect, I received a most salutary lesson from U Thant.

After my general education in France, I had studied economics at the University of Heidelberg, law at Strasbourg, and again economics at Columbia University. What I had learned helped me to better understand what was going on in the world, but somehow I had the impression that law professors and economists were trying to establish a kind of monopoly, a science that wanted to encompass everything while protecting itself from outside influences, a discipline that tried to explain all human affairs and in reality explained very little.

After a while, I decided not to bury myself in books and reviews in which obscure professors argued endlessly with each other about abstract laws, curves, or mathematical formulas, which seemed to me so far from reality.

Life was too beautiful to be wasted in such a somber field. However, even at the UN, one had to adhere to the last retrenchment of the specialists: the jargon. If you do not use the jargon of the jurists, economists, or of some other profession, you will be expelled from the club, for you have violated the most sacred rule of the game: the language. Without jargon, dogmas, and excommunication, interest groups believe that they cannot survive.

One of my first assignments when I joined U Thant was speech writing. I soon discovered that neither my legal nor my economic background had prepared me for such a task. The first speech he asked me to write was intended for Asian people. It had to deal with human problems, political trends, cultures, the concerns, aspirations, and soul of the common people — in short, with basic, simple, understandable issues. Only when it came to the economic part of the speech was I really at ease. I prepared a first draft that left me very unhappy, but U Thant insisted on seeing it during the weekend, for he wanted to begin working on the speech himself. I gave it to him reluctantly and thereby earned myself one of the most excruciating lessons of my life. On Monday morning, he returned the draft to me with the following annotation:

"A commendable attempt, but the quality is uneven and at times too wordy and even high-faluting. I want to have another look at it after the final draft."

Good God, what a lesson that was! Having gone through three universities on two continents, having had a long career and experience at the UN, having dealt with a large variety of world problems, and still to be unable to write a satisfactory speech for the Secretary General!

During the day he asked me to join him in his office to further discuss the speech. Among his remarks, one still sticks in my mind like a dart. Pointing at a sentence, he asked:

"What does this mean: the 'economies of scale'?"

I explained it to him and he remarked:

"Well, if you can explain it so simply, why don't you say so in the text? I am a simple man and I will speak to simple people. If I do not understand what I am saying, they will not understand me either. I feel that one ought to be straightforward if one wants to create better world understanding."

I have never forgotten that heaven-sent lesson. It put me back on the right track. U Thant was absolutely right. There is nothing important on earth that cannot be explained in simple terms. And if it can't, it is not worth speaking about, for it is irrelevant to human needs.

I drew several positive conclusions from my unfortunate experience. First, I was happy to discover that in the highest political positions there are persons who place simple, basic human values far above the claims and arrogance of experts and specialists. I got another proof of that when I worked with Secretary General Waldheim.

Second, I had to divest myself totally of any specialization and return to the good old values taught to me during my youth.

Third, in order to assist the Secretary General as best I could, I had to keep in touch with the essential trends and developments in all human affairs. It was not because it seemed impossible that I should not try; quite the contrary.

Fourth, in order to reach the people, I had to subdue the intellect and turn on the heart.

Where there is a will, there is a way. I discovered that a truly Copernican knowledge of the world and human affairs existed right under my nose at the United Nations and in its numerous specialized agencies. All I had to do was to set aside big, learned books and read faithfully the daily documents published by the UN. They gave me the best possible panorama of the state of the world, its problems and upcoming trends. I also made it a point to meet the best, most inquisitive and forward-looking UN officials, to listen to them, and to have my attention drawn to whatever they felt was important.

To fill remaining gaps and make the general reviews recommended by Descartes, I invited scientists and prominent people to luncheon and went to lectures organized by various UN departments on major world issues. I thus discovered that the expansion of the human mind and heart into all essential fields of knowledge and concern was easy, that it can be a true joy, and that the UN was the greatest school of humanism, universalism, and global knowledge that ever existed on earth. I became simultaneously a student, a teacher, a practitioner, and a man of sentiment.

Through his insistence on simplicity, U Thant had made me again the total, well-balanced, and happy human being I had been when I was an adolescent. I had no sleepless nights anymore because I had not read the latest issue of the *American Economic Review*!

I later discovered a corollary to the virtue of simplicity — namely, that of superficiality. It was a former deputy mayor of New York City, Timothy Costello, who opened my mind to it. I was to deliver a luncheon speech to a meeting of CIRCLE, a New York cultural and civic organization. Mr. Costello, now president of Adelphi University, was seated next to me. During the luncheon, he complained about the superficiality with which a college president has to treat so many fields of knowledge and education. He said:

"I am a psychologist and I cannot wait for the day when I will be able to return to my specialty and dig myself into it." I commented wryly:

"Dear Mr. Costello, in my view it takes a lot of courage to be superficial. The man who buries himself in his specialty often closes his eyes to the more general streams of life and knowledge. His specialization can become resignation and an escape from the difficulties of grasping the total order of things. The world continues to turn, knowledge to expand, humanity to grow, while specialists keep on building protective walls around them. They may wake up someday and discover that the winds of change have blown their specialty to pieces. We surely need specialists, for the march of science will proceed farther and farther into the infinitely large and small, but we need also generalists and universalists that is, people who have the courage to know the essentials of all sciences and see the totality. Superficiality can be a duty. In any event, it is certainly a form of courage."

Mr. Costello looked at me, highly amused, and he observed with a twinkle in his eyes:

"You made my day! I cannot wait until I repeat your sentence to my Board next week: 'It takes a lot of courage to be superficial.'"

If I include this anecdote in the subject of happiness, it is because a good part of my life has been made miserable by professors, superiors, and experts who always told me what I should read, think, believe, or do in order to get society's approval and applause, while instinctively I knew that it was not so and that life was infinitely more beautiful and richer than all their theories, disciplines, and specialties. In my view, the survival, enlightenment, and constant enrichment of a science requires the broadest possible opening toward total life and all other branches of knowledge. Universities begin to recognize it, but again as a special "discipline" called by such ugly names as

"cybernetics," "systems analysis," "multidisciplinary," "supradiscipli-
nary," "transdisciplinary," etc.

However specialized a person may be, for the sake of his own happiness and achievement, he must always remain a warm, passionate
being, with both mind and heart wide open to all great streams of life
and knowledge. His aperture must range from the infinitely small to
the infinitely large, his heart must embrace all peoples, races, and living creatures on earth. Each of us is a Copernicus, a Faust, a
Leonardo, provided he is a universal being standing far above the
fractured and competing claims of specialists, interest groups, institutions, nations, religions, or ideologies, which all too often claim
sanctity, sovereignty, and infallibility, practice intolerance, and belittle
us through narrow allegiance under the menace of excommunication.

Whatever his profession or specialization may be, each human has
been blessed with eyes to see, ears to hear, a brain to think, a heart to
love, and a soul to encompass the entire world and universe. It is by
putting all his senses and passion into it that a person aggrandizes his
life and profession and sees his proper, happy place in a well-under-
stood total order of things.

Of course, I do not feel entirely at ease with my advocacy of superficiality, although an analogy with physical science reassures me
somewhat. The human eye receives at any moment more than one
hundred million bits of information, registered by rods and cones in
the retina. These light waves are transformed into electrical impulses,
which are reduced by ganglions in the optical nerve to one million
units of information. These data are further reduced and analyzed by
the brain and transformed into images and conclusions for storage,
or into commands given to the various parts of the body through the
nervous system. The process of abstraction, rejection, summarizing,
synthesis, and simplification is therefore very fundamental to human
life in order to cope with our planet's infinite complexity. Perhaps
"superficiality" is not the right word, but there is the fact that we see
and love a "beautiful" woman as an entity and not as the trillions of
cells and miles of vessels of which she is made. Beauty, ugliness,
peace, justice, order, life, death, good, evil, and happiness are all bold

abstractions and simplifications resorted to by humans in order to survive in the bewildering complexity surrounding us. The leader, the captain, the chief, the head is the one who draws the right conclusion from all the confusion and decides on the best course of action. He is the audacious simplifier who sees the fundamental currents in a sea of information. Similarly, to lead our own lives we need to simplify, synthesize, and adhere to a few basic luminous concepts and principles. The higher the principles on the scale of human values, the richer our lives will be.

The Need for Poets

The heart has its reasons, which reason ignores.

In January 1973, the president of Lions International, Mr. Georges Friedrichs, paid a visit to Secretary General Kurt Waldheim and offered the United Nations the co-operation of his organization on global issues such as the environment, the world's handicapped, and the international drug problem. The Secretary General asked me to take the necessary steps to enlist the support of this important non-governmental association, which has twentynine thousand clubs and more than one million members. Mr. Friedrichs was a compatriot of mine. He came from the French city of Annecy, which has inspired several great masterpieces of world literature, among others Jean-Jacques Rousseau's works and the Spiritual Exercises of St. Francis de Sales. I asked him:

"Speaking of the environment, how is your city's beautiful lake faring? Has it kept its marvelous purity or has it turned green and polluted like Lake Geneva, which in the late 1960s was in a critical stage?"[1]

He answered:

"Thanks to a group of fishermen from villages around the lake, and to the deputy mayor of Annecy, a doctor who is deeply in love with nature, preventive action has been taken as early as 1957, long before the UN Stockholm Conference on the environment. They created an intercommunal syndicate of riparian localities, which built a circular sewer all around the lake in order to prevent any pollution

[1]Since then, Lake Geneva has found again most of its original purity, due to the efforts of its riparians.

from reaching it. Due to this foresight, our lake is one of the purest in Europe, and in 1972 we were awarded the European Prize for the protection of the environment. If you are interested in our efforts, I will gladly send you some material."

I was very interested indeed. Among the documentation I received was a book entitled *The Life of an Alpine Lake: Chronicle of the Protection of Lake Annecy* by Dr. Servettaz, the deputy mayor of Annecy. That book gave me the clue of the miracle that had saved the lake: A poet had concluded an alliance with fishermen, an act of love had inspired the right action and foresight long before any scientific and selfish considerations regarding the environment created a world uproar. Dr. Servettaz had transcended his thorough hydrological and ecological knowledge into a poetic relation with the beauty and purity of the lake. The findings of his mind were aggrandized by the warmth of his heart. It confirmed my old belief that poetry, love, vision, and dream are often infinitely more perceptive in devising the right course of action than scientific, economic, and political considerations. It made me wish that next to each chief of state and in each international organization there should be poets and artists to inspire human guidance with the eyes and the voice of the heart and not solely reason. Alas, the time is not yet ripe. Among the vast documentation prepared for the world conferences on the seas, water, and the deserts, there are no poems or songs. Among the experts who attend these conferences there are no poets or artists. How sad this is, when one thinks of all the love the seas, water, and the deserts have engendered in the hearts of humans from time immemorial. What would the great kings of the past, who were surrounded by poets and artists, say if they saw our world run only by experts, scientists, and politicians?

But one cannot speak too far ahead of one's time, for anyone who does passes for a fool. We still live in an essentially material, intellectual, and science-imbued society. In world affairs too, the language of reason dismally predominates that of the heart. Thus, in a speech titled "The UN: The Least Powerful and Most Influential Organization on Earth," in August 1973, I presented the problem as follows:

Let me give you the examples of two European lakes, not far from each other, Lake Geneva and Lake Annecy, to show you what courses the world can take. Both were crystal-clear a few years ago. Around Lake Geneva nobody thought that the individual wrongdoings of riparian villages and cities could ever harm the lake. Nothing was done among the surrounding communities to act in concert and it was only when the lake had deteriorated that a riparian association was created. In Annecy, on the contrary, due to the wisdom of a doctor and of fishermen, such an association was established as early as 1957 and a circular sewer was built, which prevents any sewage from reaching the lake. The Annecy lake has preserved its beautiful, crystal-clear water. Foresight, care, and co-operation were the secrets, and the same applies to the world.

The United Nations is an association of interested governments, located around the seas and oceans and sharing in the management and administration of our planet's resources. If, like the villagers around Lake Annecy, governments come to the United Nations with less concern about politics and narrow interests and more concern for the world's broader interests, if they work together and wisely manage resources in which all mankind has a stake, then we will see — at long last — permanent peace on this planet.

But Dr. Servettaz was infinitely more to the point when he spoke of love, beauty, sentiment, emotion, happiness. It was his love for the lake that saved this jewel of nature in its resplendent crown of mountains. He proved that love and poetry were infinitely better guides for the right action than all the science and intelligence of this world.

The United Nations Environment Conference met in Stockholm in 1972. It gave birth to the United Nations Environment Program, which follows worldwide the good example of Lake Annecy: several treaties, conferences, and instruments among riparian states today try to safeguard the seas and oceans, these internal lakes of our world. Many good actions have been undertaken by scores of experts, scientists, economists, administrators, and political men from many nations and cities.

But where are the poets, the artists, the voices of the heart and the soul, which alone can elevate humanity above its current material and intellectual state? A world in which a poem submitted to an international conference raises eyebrows is a world that has still a long way to go in its pursuit of beauty, love, and happiness. Poetry and art are not useless: They are the keenest perceptions of the mysteries of life on this planet.

The story of Dr. Servettaz sometimes reminds me of two other men who held similar views regarding the conduct of human affairs: Einstein and Freud. I am referring to their famous exchange of letters in 1932 on the ways of freeing mankind from the menace of war.[2] Einstein was convinced that with the advance of modern science this issue was a matter of life and death for civilization. Alas, for all the zeal displayed, every attempt at its solution had ended in a lamentable breakdown. So he turned to Freud, whom he asked if man's instinctive life had any bearing on the problem and could offer a basis for new and fruitful modes of action. Freud, in a memorable letter, gave him this luminous answer:

". . . human instincts are of two kinds: those that conserve and unify, which we call 'erotic' (in the meaning Plato gives to Eros in his *Symposium*) . . . ; and second, the instincts to destroy and kill, which we assimilate as the aggressive or destructive instincts. These are, as you perceive, the well-known opposites, Love and Hate, transformed into theoretical entities; they are, perhaps, another aspect of those eternal polarities, attraction and repulsion, which fall within your province. . . ." And he concludes that peace and nonviolence can only be achieved by "developing the love instincts" and "by the transfer of power to a larger combination, founded on the community of sentiments linking up its members." Therefore, despite its shortcomings, he held the League of Nations to be a unique and hopeful development in human evolution:

[2]*Einstein on Peace*, ed. Otto Nathan and Heinz Norden (New York: Schocken Books, 1968).

"... we should be taking a very shortsighted view of the League of Nations were we to ignore the fact that here is an experiment the like of which has rarely — never before, perhaps, on such a scale — been attempted in the course of history. It is an attempt to acquire the authority (in other words, coercive influence), which hitherto reposed exclusively in the possession of power, by calling into play certain idealistic attitudes of mind," including "ties of sentiment" or "identifications" between the members of the group as opposed to violent compulsion.

This text should be meditated upon by all anthropologists, sociologists, and political men of our time. It is almost identical to the principles advocated by U Thant as the only long-term solution to the problems of war and peace. What Freud said about the League of Nations is even truer today of the United Nations. Here again the views of Einstein, Freud, and U Thant are in complete harmony. If such great people held the same convictions, there must be a deep-seated truth in them. Instead of the thousands of books published each year on "political science," "power," "national interests," "conflicts," "negotiation," "diplomacy," and "international affairs," it would be infinitely better to teach love, sentiment, beauty, purity, and truthfulness as the ways of human civilization. Then we would at long last see crystallize the ultimate and largest "combination founded on the community of sentiments linking up its members," namely, a world human community of all men, women, and children of this planet, bound together in flesh, mind, heart, and spirit.

Pablo Casals on Alcohol

Nothing is more apt to contribute to human happiness than abstention from alcohol.

Each of us knows perfectly well what damage alcohol can inflict upon mind and body. From personal experience, I can only say that the happiest mornings in my life were those succeeding days of total abstinence and my most miserable ones those following days of abuse. There is nothing more beautiful in life than a "clean morning," after a day without smoking or alcohol, and after a good night's sleep. Then man's faculties, bestowed upon him by God or by millions of years of evolution, left undisturbed, are sharp and sure like a razor's edge. Man is in full harmony with the great streams and mysteries of life surrounding him. Body, brain, heart, and soul are at their peak and optimum conditions are fulfilled to enjoy happiness. Clear waters, limpid skies, a child's smile, a cathedral's spire, a beautiful woman's face, these are the images I associate in my mind with a glorious morning following days of total abstinence.

In addition to personal experience, what impressed me most regarding this subject was the following anecdote concerning Pablo Casals.

The date was April 1970, and the place was the UN Secretariat building in New York. It was one of U Thant's last years as Secretary General. He had still several cherished unfulfilled dreams. One of them was to have a United Nations hymn composed by his great friend, Pablo Casals. The two men loved and respected each other dearly. For U Thant, Casals' music was the boundless and supreme expression of his own dreams and aspirations for peace. In Pablo's eyes, U Thant and the United Nations were the practical and earthly incarnations of these dreams. Every encounter between the two men was a moving experience, as many people could see from the famous television program of Pablo Casals' performance of his UN hymn in the General Assembly hall on October 24, 1971: They fell into each other's arms; Pablo Casals was crying and uttering the words "peace, peace," while U Thant was murmuring to him, "My dear maestro, I am so happy, you are a great man, a very kind man. . . ."

Pablo Casals had come to New York at the behest of U Thant to give a fund-raising concert for the benefit of the United Nations International School. The Secretary General gave a cocktail party in his honor on the thirty-eighth floor of the UN Secretariat building. Among the guests was Leopold Stokowski, the conductor, a neighbor of U Thant in Riverdale.

After the usual welcoming embrace between U Thant and Casals and the handshakes and presentations, beverages were offered. I was talking to Pablo Casals when a waitress neared us with a tray of glasses filled with champagne. Pablo Casals, whose eyes were blinking under a bright light, asked her:

"What is it?"

She answered with a smile:

"It is just lemonade."

He seized a glass and was about to bring it to his lips when his wife hastened toward him, took the cup from his hand, tasted the liquid, and said:

"This is champagne! You cannot drink it." And she walked away with the cup.

Thereupon, Pablo Casals told me the following story:

"When I was a young man, I once went to see my doctor and told him that I was feeling a kind of laziness in my fingers. After a thorough examination, he asked me: 'Do you drink?' I answered negatively, but added that like all Spaniards I had a glass of wine at luncheon and at dinner. He then said: 'Well, if you want to become a great, renowned artist and avoid that laziness in your fingers, you must never touch again a drop of wine or alcohol.' I obeyed him faithfully during all my life."

I looked with admiration at the ninety-four-year-old maestro. In front of me stood a man whose fingers were still agile and divine, a human being whose clear brain and heart were to give the world a year later a hymn worthy of Beethoven's "Choral to Joy," and who had had the strength and perseverance to abstain from alcohol for three quarters of a century! The words of a Hindu saying came to my mind:

"To give pleasure to others, the artist must deprive himself of all pleasures."

I was so impressed that ever since then I have tried to follow Pablo Casals' example, perhaps less strictly and successfully, but nevertheless with constancy. I could never forget Pablo Casals' words and his living demonstration of what abstinence from alcohol can do for the physical, mental, and affective fitness of a human being.

During my travels around the world, I have learned that what is true of individuals also applies to societies. There are on this earth nations that are slowly but surely drinking themselves to death. They wonder why their health, vitality, confidence, happiness, and optimism are withering away, but cannot visualize for a moment that it might be due to abuse of alcohol. And there are others that, owing to moderation or abstinence, are preparing themselves for greatness and leadership in the world. Indeed, this is how it should be.

Some scientists believe that average human life lies between one hundred and two hundred years, provided the environment is ideal — that is, at a coefficient of one. Alcohol and smoking are two of the main factors that reduce that coefficient. Individuals, nations, and the international community must therefore set for themselves, as one of their primary environmental goals, the control of these two new epidemics, which inflict such damage on the human race. According to the World Health Organization, alcohol and tobacco are drugs. They diminish the marvelous body and mind we have inherited from evolution. If we want to build a better world, we must stop debilitating and destroying ourselves. No drink or drug on earth can ever bring happiness, for happiness is an internal disposition of man that requires the optimum functioning of his body, mind, heart, and soul.

Pablo Casals' experience was a living illustration of the first of U Thant's four principles for happiness: respect for physical life and for the human body. After almost three million years of human evolution, we are witnessing only now the birth of a true science of nutrition or optimum nourishment of man. Nothing indeed is more apt to give humans longer, healthier, and happier lives than the right intakes of food, liquids, and air. And the same applies to mental, moral, and spiritual nourishment, for which we do not yet possess the rudiments of a science.

Pablo Casals was infinitely more than a musician of genius. He was also a great life-impassioned man who felt that he had unique duties toward life in return for the gift God had given him. Two years later, when Sri Chinmoy, Director of the United Nations Meditation Group, interviewed him in Puerto Rico — Pablo Casals was then ninety-six years old — he exclaimed:

> . . . The child must know that he is a miracle, a miracle, that since the beginning of the world there hasn't been and until the end of the world there will not be another child like him. He is a unique thing, a unique thing, from the beginning until the end of the world. Now, that child acquires a responsibility: "Yes, it is true, I am a miracle. I am a miracle like a tree is a miracle, like a flower is a miracle. Now, if I am a miracle, can I do a bad thing? I can't, because I am a miracle, I am a miracle."
>
> God, Nature. I call God, Nature, or Nature, God. And then comes the other thought: "I am a miracle that God or Nature has done. Could I kill? Could I kill someone? No, I can't. Or another human being who is a child like me, can he kill me?" I think that this theory can help to bring forth another way of thinking in the world. The world of today is bad; it is a bad world. And it is because they don't talk to the children in the way that the children need.

Casals, like most great men of this world, had discovered the secret of secrets — namely, that each human life is a miracle, a unique, unrepeatable prodigy in the universe. And like U Thant, he drew this sacred conclusion: Humans should never destroy or diminish life, neither their own nor that of their brothers and sisters.

My Lambarene

Be faithful to your love and you will be recompensed beyond measure.

One of the persons who possesses the most lucid and intelligent comprehension of the United Nations is Norman Cousins. His humanism, his lifelong endeavors for world peace and understanding, his efforts at reconciliation between East and West, his denunciations of all injustices and irresponsible behaviors on our planet, his writings and public pronouncements, his untiring encounters with statesmen and exhortations to them, his unfaltering support for the first budding world organization, his endless patience at listening to all persons of good will, his inspiration to others and his encouragement of anyone who has a dream for peace and progress count among the greatest services any man has ever rendered in a single lifetime. He is one of the few men on earth in whom I have confided my wildest dreams and hopes for humanity. After each of our encounters, I feel aggrandized and reinvigorated. Never would he say what so many others readily throw at the face of peacemakers or think silently behind their backs: "You are not realistic. You are an idealist, a dreamer, a fool. Nothing of what you hope will ever come true." Norman Cousins is always on the side of those who are rolling stones uphill to build a cathedral, however often they may fail or falter.

The following anecdote illustrates the type of strength and encouragement he so generously provides others.

In January of 1972, after a decade of service, U Thant left the United Nations and was succeeded by Mr. Waldheim. The immediate collaborators of U Thant did not know what their fate would be. I scarcely knew Mr. Waldheim, whom I had met only occasionally when he was the permanent representative of Austria to the UN. My future was quite uncertain. I had been appointed to U Thant's personal staff on the understanding that it would not commit his successor.

In the midst of my incertitude, Norman Cousins came to see me. At Christmas I had sent him my usual year-end reflections on the state of the world as well as a few ideas for initiatives that could be taken during the new year. I had suggested to him the creation of a world publishing house (which would publish U Thant's memoirs to start with), the launching of a world magazine devoted to our planet's global problems, and the holding of world public-opinion polls on some of the major world issues.

He came to my office at the UN and said to me:

"Robert, I had the same idea as you and have decided to create a world magazine. I come to offer to you to be its managing editor."

"Me? Editor of a magazine? Good Lord, but I have never set foot in a newspaper! It is a world totally foreign to me. I cannot tell you how deeply touched I am by your offer and how good you make me feel at this moment, but how on earth did it occur to you to think of me for your magazine?"

"I know that you are not familiar with the publishing world, but I will take care of that. I thought of you because I need a man who is fond of the world and of its people, someone who can bring us a step forward on the road to peace. I have canvassed my mind and I came up with one name at the top of my list — yours."

I protested vehemently, but he went on:

"I have observed you, I know you well. Like your compatriot Albert Schweitzer, you are conditioned by your double culture. You cannot be different from what you are. But you must now come to your own. In the United Nations you will forever remain an anonymous official, unable to write, to publish, to make yourself known. In my world you will be free. I offer you a magazine for the expression of your ideas."

I looked through the window of my office and contemplated the vast horizon of dwellings, roads, and chimneys on Long Island. A boat was passing on the East River, saluting the United Nations with a whistle blow. Norman Cousins was opening an entirely new vista to me. He was right. Here I would remain an anonymous official among many others, respectful of the political and institutional constraints imposed on my ideas. How could I say no to such a luminous offer, which would open an entirely new phase in my life? But deep in my heart I was hearing a different language. I resorted to a quick compromise and asked for time to think:

"Dear Norman, a person must always listen to his first instinct when he is presented with a new situation in life. My heart tells me that I should not leave this organization, in which I have placed all my soul. My mind tells me the contrary. I will most likely follow my heart and decline your generous offer for reasons I do not yet see clearly. I promise though to consider it carefully and to consult my family. The turmoil you have created in me must subside. I am unable to think well at this moment. In any event, whatever the outcome may be, you will never know how much your confidence means to me just now."

A few days passed. I examined the offer calmly from every possible point of view, and discussed it with my wife who, as usual, left me complete freedom of decision. Norman Cousins was matching all financial conditions of the UN. Nevertheless, my heart, mind, and instinct coalesced to tell me that I should stay with the United Nations. I had devoted practically all my life to the world organization. I was happy, very happy in my work. How could I be unfaithful to such a marriage of love? I had to stay until the very end and see what a lifetime of world public service would mean to me. I would simply not be able to bring myself to divorce the UN.

A few days later I went to see Norman Cousins to give him my reply.

He had an office across the street from the UN, at the Church Center. While I was waiting in the reception room, I looked out of the window and saw the great UN building in front of me. Its flags were waving in the winter wind. It stood there, all blue and gray, a symbol of human dreams and hopes, its round, flattened General Assembly cupola clinging closely to the earth, as if mindful of the interests of its diverse peoples, its tall Secretariat building reaching toward the sky, as if to express the dream of human unity. High up there, on the thirty-eighth floor, the little being that I was had an office. Mankind allowed me to work there every day, to deal with the hopes of the world and its people, and to pour out my passion for life and for our beautiful planet. How could my answer be but negative? What fortune, what glory could ever match such rare privilege?

I therefore said to Norman Cousins a few moments later:

"What you are seeking above all is my knowledge of the world. You know perfectly well that alone, by myself, I am nobody. All I have to offer I have learned in that blue-and-gray building. Only there can I get a proper view of the state, the heart, and the longings of the world. Only there can I discern its destiny and listen to the heartbeats, dreams, sufferings, and mournings of all peoples of the world. If I cross that street, I will lose instantly most of what I have. No; I cannot leave the UN, I cannot cross that street. I must stay in that fragile temple of hope of humanity, where there unfolds one of the greatest adventures ever of the human race: the birth of a global society, the march toward a total understanding of man's place on his planet and in the universe. You mentioned Albert Schweitzer and his double culture. He left Alsace to seek the human soul under different faces, races, and climates, and to help and heal against the most incredible odds. I too have left my fatherland to seek the human soul under various faces, cultures, and beliefs. I too want to help and heal against the most impossible odds. The United Nations is my Lambarene, as it was U Thant's Bô tree, or place of enlightenment. I am a helper among many anonymous helpers. I promise you to always keep my knowledge at your disposal, for I have no greater desire than to see *World Magazine* become a great success so that it may help us in our struggle for a peaceful, better, and more beautiful world."

Norman Cousins understood well the language of the heart. We remained great friends. *World Magazine* became a fine review, a gallant advocate of global co-operation, and a stanch supporter of the United Nations. Its success proved how little I was needed. For my part, I stayed in my Lambarene of sorrows and pains, in the great house of hope of humanity, faithful to my peace-serving job. And I remained forever grateful to Norman Cousins for the confidence he had placed in me at a moment when I needed it most.

Mazzone, or the Faith of a Great Artist

One day, on my way to the United Nations, I saw in the window of a gallery in New York City a most extraordinary exposition of sculptures. There were powerful bronzes of Christopher Columbus, Toscanini, Cardinal Cooke; white marbles of nudes projecting themselves toward heaven in magnificent movements of joy; peaceful, classical Florentine busts of unknown persons; and several white plasters, among which a pathetic Christ hanging from a pole, his two hands tied together above the head, sagged down in a dramatic gesture of death and despair. I thought to myself:

"Is it possible that there still exists such an artist in our epoch of largely decomposed and disarticulated art? Who is this wouldbe Michelangelo lost in our twentieth century? How can a man have such a strong belief in himself?"

An open book in the window told the story of the artist. It showed pictures of his mother and father from Puglia in the South of Italy. He had had no formal art training and was a simple stonecutter who had found in himself the urge to sculpt and to mold with his hands. He worked with some of the master sculptors of Italy and later came to America with no lesser an ambition than to be recognized as the leading sculptor of the twentieth century.

I stopped in front of that window every morning as long as the display lasted, deriving from its sight great strength for my own work at the United Nations. This man had an incomparable, intuitive grasp of the greatness and drama of life. His sculptures reflected the eternal trilogy of creation, preservation, and destruction. Each bust expressed the deepest characteristics and aspirations of the sculpted person. His Christ in particular engraved itself profoundly on my mind. I had always wanted to have a Christ in my office at the United Nations, but it had to be a very special, a very beautiful and meaningful Christ. Mazzone's Christ was extraordinarily moving and beautiful. What a dream if it could someday adorn my office and inspire my daily work! But alas, this was only a dream, for I would never be able to afford such a masterpiece.

I wanted to make the acquaintance of the artist who carried such a strong message in himself. He would be ideally suited to give expression to mankind's dreams for peace, justice, progress, and beauty. I jotted down his name and address and told my secretary that I would write to him.

But in the turmoil of daily affairs such laudable intentions always receive lowest priority. Art and beauty are not main preoccupations of our time. For one artist, there are dozens of economic consultants or other experts who knock at the door of the United Nations. It is true that food, health, and shelter deserve priority, but artistic production and creativity too can offer happiness to the most humble creatures on earth.

Several months passed and I never wrote to the sculptor. The display of his works in Manhattan ended, and all that was left in my mind was the powerful impression of his sculptures, above all that of his Christ.

Then one day I found on my desk a large envelope addressed to me by "Mazzone, sculptor, Jersey City." I thought I was dreaming, and I asked my secretary if by any chance I had written to him. I had intended to, but never did. The thought of telepathy crossed my mind, but the answer was much simpler: Monsignor Giovanetti, the observer of the Holy See at the United Nations, had advised Mazzone to write to me in order to convey to Secretary General U Thant his wish to sculpt a bust of him. This time I seized the telephone and called the artist at his studio:

"Mr. Mazzone, I know you well. I admired your work for many days at your display and I intended to get in touch with you. You seem to carry in yourself a very special message, which is close to the ideals of the United Nations. I am sorry that I have not written to you as I intended, but Fate has corrected my negligence since you have now written to me."

I told him also of the profound impression his Christ had left on me: "I will never forget the image of this tormented plaster body hanging against the background of rough sack material."

A few days later Mazzone came to my office at the United Nations. He held an elongated object in his arms, reminding me of a covered machine gun! He unwrapped it carefully: It was a replica of his crucifix! He offered it to me with these words:

"I hope you will like this copy of my Christ. I made it especially for you. May God help you in your work as He does in mine."

This took place early in 1971. Today I could write a book about Mazzone. He has taught me so much about art and life. Above all, he has sustained my own faith with his unfaltering enthusiasm and zest for life. Often, in the evening, when I feel tired and discouraged after a troublesome day, I call Mazzone and I hear him say:

"Mr. Muller, I will never get discouraged, *mamma mia!* Life is so beautiful, even when I do not have one dollar in my pocket. You will see, everything will be all right."

When people hear me speak so optimistically about the future of the world, they have someone in front of them who is often reinvigorated by Mazzone's tenacious courage and faith. When I do not see him for a while, his Christ in my office reminds me that man should never give up hope in his struggle for justice, peace, and beauty.

Today, two magnificent busts of U Thant adorn the UN International School in New York and the Peace Museum in Menton, France. Mazzone has created numerous priceless works dealing with United Nations subjects. U Thant, like me, fell in love with him, and one of U Thant's last joys was to learn that his bust had been unveiled at the International School shortly before his death.

Perhaps I was able to be of some help to Mazzone by prompting him relentlessly to sculpt mankind's highest ideals of peace, brotherhood, friendship, help, co-operation, love, faith, liberty, and solidarity. He always came out with the straight, simple, and beautiful answer of the great poets and artists. When I challenged him to express happiness, he equated it with six basic feelings in a series of bas-reliefs reproduced on tinplates sold today in gift shops all over the United States. His perceptions were:

Happiness is being a mother.
Happiness is being a father.
Happiness is being brothers.
Happiness is being sisters.
Happiness is being a grandfather.
Happiness is being a grandmother.

In these lapidary statements he had defined happiness infinitely better than I. Hanging on a wall or standing on a cupboard, his bas-reliefs procure today more joy to more people than any lengthy philosophical works. My pride and consolation is that Mazzone's famous series on happiness might have never seen the light of day if I had not encouraged him to create it.

I hold only one thing against that artist: He is the only man on earth who made me regret that I was not rich. I have never labored for wealth or fame, since God has blessed me with a good body and mind, with a wonderful family, and with the most satisfying job in the world. But since I have known Mazzone, I have often thought that, if I were rich, I would lock him up in a studio and make him work day and night, as the Florentine rulers did, in order to extract from his divine hands the greatest possible number of immortal sculptures.

Uncle Sylvain Bloch

Always place yourself in the position of your human brother.

America has been a favorite destination for emigrants from Alsace-Lorraine. A first exodus took place after the 1870 Franco-German War, when Germany annexed the two provinces. It then continued as part of the German immigration to the United States until 1914. Finally, in the 1930s, many Jews from Alsace-Lorraine left for America when they feared that Nazi Germany might take over all of Europe.

As a result, a large colony of Alsace-Lorrainers settled in America, especially in New York. One of the strongest French associations in the city is the Union Alsacienne. Many Alsatians and Lorrainers have been very successful in America. The great Statue of Liberty, which greets visitors and immigrants in New York Harbor, is the work of an Alsatian, Bartholdi. The original models for the huge statue are still at Colmar in Alsace. The word "America" was born in that region when a monk from Freiburg came to Alsace to have the voyages of Amerigo Vespucci printed by Martin Waldseemuller in 1507 in St. Dié. He decided to call the newly discovered continent provisionally "America." In recognition of that fact, the American people reconstructed the city of St. Dié, burned to the ground by German SS on Christmas Eve of 1944 under the horrified eyes of the population, which had been forced out of their houses into the snowy hills. One of the two remaining copies of the monk's book is still on display in the public library of the little town of Selestat near Colmar. Roger Wallach was a chemical engineer from Mulhouse who immigrated to the United States in 1914 in order to avoid being enlisted in the German army. He brought with him the secret of khaki coloring, which was very valuable to the American army, and later he invented one of the most popular products of this century: cellophane. I have already spoken of the success in the United States of Dr. Émile Coué, the famous doctor-psychologist from Nancy. Shortly after my arrival in the United States I was invited to one of the yearly balls organized by the Alsatian Union in the Statler Hilton. There I met a gray-haired gentleman named Seltzer. He had come from Alsace to the United States many years ago as an intern in a pharmaceutical firm. He stayed in America, became very successful, and introduced in the United States several pharmaceutical products from his home region, among them Alka-Seltzer and the unguent of Dr. Bengué. He asked me:

"Do you remember the balm your mother used to put on your chest when you were a child to prevent the flu? She applied it also, I am sure, on the limbs of your father when he had rheumatism. The cream smelled strongly, like camphor. Do you remember?"

Indeed, I remembered very well. It could be found in practically every home. I had to live with its odor through the long winter, and I remember very vividly how my mother used to massage my father's back, her hands dripping with the shiny and greasy camphor.

"Well, it was Dr. Bengué's balm," said Mr. Seltzer. "I introduced it in the United States together with several other products from the homeland."

Mr. Seltzer died a few years later. He was, with Albert Schweitzer, one of the most prominent Alsatians I met in New York.

Among the Alsatian Jews who settled in Manhattan, the man to whom I owe most in my career is Henry S. Bloch, a former director at the United Nations. He was one of my first superiors in the world organization. Seldom has there been a man who has taught so much to his younger collaborators. He stimulated us constantly, pinpointing and correcting our weaknesses, making independent, strong, and thinking individuals of each of us. A good number of the present directors at the UN come from the small fiscal and financial branch that he headed. He later became commissioner for technical assistance and worked closely with Dag Hammarskjöld, especially in the Congo, but he finally resigned from the UN, to the great regret of the

Secretary General and of his colleagues, and joined the investment firm of Warburg and Co. in Wall Street.

We remained very close friends, almost brothers, both as former UN colleagues and as Alsace-Lorrainers. One day, he called me and asked whether I could pay a visit to his uncle, Sylvain Bloch, who had been hospitalized at Mount Sinai in Manhattan. Uncle Sylvain had taken care of Henry Bloch as a child after his father had been killed in World War I. Before immigrating to the United States, Sylvain Bloch had lived in Strasbourg, where he owned a famous brandy factory called La Cigogne (the Stork), which produced a line of well-known Alsatian liqueurs: kirsch, mirabelle, framboise, quetsch. He was now retired and very old. His doctor and his nephew feared the worst for him.

I joined Henry Bloch at the hospital. Uncle Sylvain was arguing vehemently with the nurses, refusing to take pills, injections, or anything else. The broad-chested, stocky man was nailed to his bed by a host of circulatory troubles. He had seldom been sick in his life. His strong nature was refusing to let go or to be tampered with. I had in front of me a real man, a fighter, a well-centered human being who must have lived an extraordinary, positive life. But he seemed to know that his end was near. Nobody could fool him with pills, needles, or good words. He flatly rejected all care, putting his last strength into that refusal. Looking attentively at him, I wondered what I could do for this vanishing giant occupied with his struggle against death. Although I barely knew him, I felt very close to him, perhaps because of his physical resemblance to his nephew, which was probably also matched by the same moral and intellectual strength. I had the impression that I knew Uncle Sylvain for a long time.

I decided to follow an old precept of my father's that U Thant later taught me anew in a subtler and more philosophical way: Always try to place yourself in the position of your human brother. I mentally espoused the man's broad, strong bodily features as well as his frame of mind. I saw myself nailed to that bed, in full possession of my senses, but knowing that I was going to die. In front of me stood a younger man from the old country. What could he do for me at such a moment? The answer came straightforward to my mind: Talk to me about the homeland.

I looked through the window overlooking Central Park.

The sun was slowly setting in a golden glory.

I said to Uncle Sylvain:

"Do you remember the sunsets at home?"

"Yes. They were beautiful! Here they are not the same. I am glad to have a piece of nature to look at in this hospital, but it is not the same. I would exchange the whole of New York for Strasbourg. Here the sunsets do not speak to my heart as they did in Alsace."

I had been brought up in a Jewish neighborhood in my home town, since my father had opened his first hatmaker's shop in the Goldgasse, the street of the Jewish gold merchants. I therefore knew well the Jewish ways. I began to speak to Uncle Sylvain in our dialect, which is very close to Yiddish. I talked about the people I had known: Bloch, the curtain manufacturer; the Weill brothers, who were food wholesalers; and good old Jacob with his club foot, who sent me frequently across the river to buy tobacco in the Saar Territory, where it was cheaper due to lower taxes. These were all mighty fine people, very respected in our town. Their forefathers had come to our region many centuries ago. They were happy people, firmly settled, and well integrated in our local community. They had not forgotten that Strasbourg and Alsace had been the first region in Europe to give the Jews a legal status in the Middle Ages. Hence their close association with the local people despite their different religion and customs.

Uncle Sylvain's mind having been set back home, he soon remembered the Weills and the Blochs and their cousins in Strasbourg. From then on, I could remain silent, listen to him, and watch him relive scenes and images from Alsace. His eyes were not looking at us anymore but were lost in the purple, peaceful sunset over Central Park. He dreamed and talked and reminisced. He said:

"We Jews were very fine people indeed over there in Alsace-Lorraine. Such decent people are difficult to find nowadays." One of the nurses returned to the room, holding a tray filled with drugs, needles, and other paraphernalia. She asked me to leave, for visiting time was over. Uncle Sylvain looked suddenly tired and weak. He gave me his hand in a soft, abandoned way. His strength and mind were else-where, across the Atlantic, somewhere in an obscure street of Strasbourg. When I left the room I had a last look at him. His eyes were lost in the sky over Central Park. I felt that I would never see him again. We had known each other only for a short time, but I had been deeply penetrated and enriched by his strong and unforgettable per-sonality.

A few days later Henry Bloch called me again. It was to tell me that Uncle Sylvain had died. When we met at the funeral home, he asked me:

"Do you know what Uncle Sylvain said to me after you left?" "I have no idea."

"He said: 'Henry, you can tell me what you want, but we can be very proud of our people. Where in the world could you find another fine man like this Jew, your friend, who just visited me? Only we can produce people like that.'"

As a Catholic, this was the most beautiful compliment I have received in my life! I felt so happy for having been able to stir some moving memories in a man who had had a full and rich life but knew that he was going to die. I was rewarded beyond measure for the lit-tle effort I had made to place myself in his position and for having talked to him about the only sensible subject that had any meaning to him: the old country.

The words of an American Indian prayer came back to my mind:

Great Spirit, grant that I may not judge my neighbor until I have walked a mile in his moccasins.

Cousin Marthe

The brain needs a stimulus to be a well-functioning central command unit for the entire being.

From a friend who is a neurologist I learned that the human brain is the last organ of the body to age: It becomes apparently more effective or "younger" over most of a person's lifetime, as it creates ever more diversified and finer chains of neurons. The human brain is an admirable, incredibly complex computer capable of branching out inwardly and of refining endlessly its capacity to store information, synthesize, summarize, conclude, and give with lightning speed instructions to the billions of parts that compose the human body. But the brain "grows" only as long as it is stimulated by the will, imagination, drive, or curiosity of the individual. Once the stimulus disappears, neurons stop growing. They atrophy and the brain loses its effectiveness as the central command unit of the human being. Disruptions and malfunctions appear in the form of all kinds of physical and psychological ills. Death not infrequently occurs after an individual has lost his will for life or basic drive. This often happens when a person retires from a very active life and is confronted with idleness and a total lack of objectives. And indeed, why should a life continue if there is no will for it?

My friend's theory offers perhaps an explanation of the mysterious phenomena of "will for happiness," "will for health," "will to succeed," "will for good," "will to love," which have intrigued me so much all my life. Curiosity and passion for life, constant learning and wanting to live may very well be the mysterious keys that switch on and command the physical, mental, moral, and cosmic fulfillment of this marvelous, intricate, complex little planet called a human being. It could be the answer to many fundamental questions regarding life and death, the fate of the individual and of social groups, and even the future of the human race.

What I had learned might have subsided from my mind after a while, as do most attempts at logical explanations of the mysteries of life, had I not been given shortly thereafter a vivid illustration of its veracity.

We were visiting in Danbury, Connecticut, a cousin of mine from Alsace-Lorraine, Marthe Bogen, who had immigrated after the war with her husband and child to the United States. My cousin Marthe is one of the most extraordinary persons I have known in my life. Few people in this world have gone through the amount of torment and miseries she and her family have suffered. Her stories would fill a sizable volume. Nevertheless, she has always remained the happiest person on earth. Her happiness engenders a tonic aureola all around her and accounts for the innumerable friends she has. One spends a few minutes with her and life is beautiful, cheerful, bouncing, exciting, full of interesting stories, and laughter. She irradiates a *joie de vivre* that catches everyone who comes near her. And of course people seek her friendship in order to benefit from this tonicity. She is quite capable of stating in a great outburst of laughter:

"Do you know the latest news? I have decided to donate my body to a medical school so that scientists and students may figure by what miracle I have survived for more than seventy years with one lung, one eye, one kidney, an artificial hip, several sectioned nerves, and a host of other minor defects. They are going to have some fun with me on the dissecting table, believe me!"

We were therefore utterly dismayed when we learned one day that she had suffered a heart attack. But she recovered soon and after her release from the hospital she invited us to her house in order to celebrate. At coffee time, I told her of my friend's theory, for it seemed to me that her whole life was a living proof of it, except for her recent heart attack.

She listened attentively, remained silent for a while, and then commented:

"My mind has been functioning at high gear while you spoke. I believe your friend is right, and I will give you a proof of it. Do you know when exactly I had my heart attack? It was on the anniversary date of the death of my husband. I was sitting here in the kitchen all day long alone, crying my soul out, and lamenting about the beautiful bygone days. I just let go. Life had no meaning for me anymore. It was worthless, purposeless. I had no reason to go on living and fighting. Living for what? For me alone? Well, at ten o'clock in the evening after several hours of such treatment, I suffered my heart attack and was taken to the hospital. What happened to me proves the correctness of your friend's theory."

Cousin Marthe's adaptation to her new condition was slow at first. She suffered three other attacks and hospitalizations. But progressively she found her good old self again, and today one can hear her once again exclaim in a cascade of laughter:

"Heart attack? What heart attack? I have seen much worse than that in my life. My heart will just be another anatomical curiosity for the students, since it is now equipped with a pacemaker. They are going to have some fun finding all the hardware located in me, I assure you! I have resumed my normal life and have erased the whole affair from my mind. The time is not yet ripe for the devil to catch me. Death may strike at any moment. We all have to go sooner or later. But I am going to resist it as long as I can. I am just not going to give in; no, sir!"

And I look at her in utter amazement. Her aged, heavy, overweight, battered, cut-up, patched-up body seems to have wings and to be animated by the spirit of a young girl who has just discovered the beauty and joys of life. Her blue, irradiating eyes are full of sunshine, flowers, and stars. She seems to have caught a piece of paradise on earth, of cosmic origin, of the cause of eternal life and resurrection.

If this can be true of an individual, it can also apply to humanity. Social groups are living entities. They require a brain, a heart, a nervous system, a will to live, an objective, a dream, an ideal. What we need most at this juncture of evolution is leaders with vision, with eyes full of peace, goodness, and a beautiful future. Humanity needs common goals, lofty goals, *joie de vivre*, and a strong belief in a peaceful, wonderful future. The worst we could ever do would be to let go, to despair, and to lose control over ourselves. We need a Cousin Marthe at the helm of each government.

VOLUME SIX

Lessons from the
United Nations

How to Deal with Pessimists

Ignore them or make them work.

One morning, after the weekly staff meeting of the Secretary General, I asked a colleague who was walking with me to the elevators:

"Well, how do you assess the current state of the world?" He answered:

"Very depressing. It seems to be getting worse every day."

"Wrong," I retorted. "How can you say that and be so pessimistic? In my view the situation is improving. Given the magnitude and complexity of human problems, we could be slaughtering each other on a worldwide scale. Yes, it could be infinitely worse. In thousands of different ways, sometimes awkwardly, tentatively, and too timidly, but always in the right general direction, humanity tries finding its way and proper place on planet Earth, and in my opinion it will succeed."

My friend answered:

"I am not surprised by your statement, for you are known as the 'optimist in residence' at the UN. But I cannot share your confidence."

I insisted:

"If we lose hope in this House of Hope, then indeed there will be no hope. As for my attitude, there are enough devil's advocates in the world. We need more people's advocates. Let me ask you this question: Suppose that overnight all remaining conflicts, from Cyprus to Vietnam through the Middle East and southern Africa were miraculously resolved and that all humans no less miraculously were guaranteed a monthly income of several thousand dollars all over the planet. Do you think that people would then be happy, that they would cease to complain, that the world would be problemless, that the newspapers would be more cheerful and positive?"

"Possibly not."

"Well, this is the crux of the matter. Humanity has simply not yet learned to be happy and to count its blessings. People all too easily forget — and are induced by the media to forget — how beautiful life really is. A balance sheet of a company lists assets and liabilities, but when it comes to the world, we see only liabilities and seldom any statements of assets and progress. The conditions on planet Earth are far from being perfect, but there has been good progress since World War II. If this has been possible, more is possible. If we have the required faith and attitude, humanity will succeed — and I believe rather soon — in ensuring permanent peace, greater justice, order, and happiness on earth. It is within our reach; I can feel it like a doctor who knows his patient, like a lover who knows his woman well. Optimism, hard work, devotion, love, and belief in the highest possible goals for humanity are the duty of all men and women of good will, especially those in this house who are paid to labor for mankind as a whole."

The elevator had arrived and our conversation ended. Moments later I was walking immersed in thoughts toward my office, with this question on my mind: "How can people render themselves unhappy through their own volition? How can one be pessimistic when life is so beautiful, so interesting, so rich, so challenging? Here is a man whom millions of people would envy for his wonderful and exciting job at the UN, blessed with so many opportunities to do good, and all he does is to complain and give up. I will never understand such people. Pessimism is beyond my comprehension. I just cannot afford it."

When I arrived at my office I found an Indian lady waiting for me: Mrs. Nigam, the president of the Federation of United Nations Associations of India. Her cheerful face was a blessing to me. Pursuing my train of thought, I asked her point-blank:

"Mrs. Nigam, are you a pessimist?"

"For heaven's sake, no! God forbid! Pessimists are second-rate people. They do not believe in life. Pessimism is just an excuse for their cowardice. All they want is to drag you down and appease their own feelings of mediocrity and fear. They come in flocks to the meetings, conferences, and ventures we organize on the UN in India. Their sole purpose is to discourage us. But I have found a simple and effective way to cope with them: I cut them right in the middle of their litanies and give them work to do. Either they leave or they work. Keep pessimists away from you or make them work, and they will not bother you. This is my recipe. It works like a charm. Try it out. Do not listen to pessimists, and pursue your good objectives."

This was a wise comment indeed. The worst thing a good person can do is to join the sad cohort of pessimists, and the next worst is to engage in a dialogue with them.

Mrs. Nigam's remark brought back to my mind a scene I had witnessed in New York shortly after the war, at a time when happiness, optimism, and belief in their country were still the dominant features of the American people. I was riding with a young Englishman in a taxicab and we were commenting about American ways of life. My companion was highly critical of what he called the naive cheerfulness of the Americans. Suddenly the taxi driver stopped his car, opened the door, and said to us:

"Young man, I have just heard enough. If you do not like it in America, go home. And keep your fare. I do not want to touch it."

I have often felt that any healthy and well-to-do earth-dweller should simply follow that taxi driver's example and say to those who unceasingly and unjustifiably complain: "If you do not like it on planet Earth, just leave it and make room for someone else who might be happy to enjoy the miracle of life."

Yes, even if there were no wars and problems, even if all humans had mountains of goods, still happiness would not reign on earth unless people felt it in themselves and made it a part of their daily lives. Happiness and not economic growth must be the ultimate objective of educators, leaders, institutions, and government. Material welfare is merely one aspect of life. The more recent aspiration for "quality of life" marks important progress but is not sufficient. Morality, love, cheerfulness, and spirituality must also be reintroduced into the scheme of life. Our objectives are simply set too low: We seek peace, justice, and high standards of living, but we do not dare to pronounce the great old words of love and happiness. There should be more sensible people like the New York taxi driver to show us the road to common sense.

UN We Believe

What is each one of us doing for peace?

There is much cynicism and discouragement on our planet nowadays, if one is to judge from the press, the media, literature, and the arts. Man's only way to keep his balance in such estrangement is to solidly root himself in his own happiness and in beliefs that continue to speak resolutely for good, peace, and justice instead of power, injustice, and violence. Such efforts cannot be wrong, for they are part of a deep-seated and immortal urge of humankind to lift itself toward ever higher levels of evolution.

My indomitable will to stay on the bright side of life in spite of the shadows and storms has derived much strength from other men and women devoting their lives to the ideals of the United Nations. I am speaking of the many nongovernmental organizations, UN associations, volunteers, and peace groups that are helping the United Nations and have been such invaluable pioneers of the global world. I will narrate here an anecdote that reflects the spirit of all of them and that shows what the determination of one or two persons can accomplish.

In October 1956, a commercial airplane of United Air Lines was flying from Denver to New York. The flight was peaceful and the world looked wonderful from far above. Suddenly the two pilots heard over their radio that trouble had broken out in Hungary. The world seemed again in danger of war. The two pilots commented on this news and deplored the sad state of the world. One of them, Captain Charles C. Dent, observed to the other, Captain Richard P. Munger:

"Perhaps it is our fault if the world is not in better shape. We always rely on others to work for peace, justice, and order, but what are we doing ourselves, each one of us? For the first time in history we have a world organization, the United Nations, but will it ever succeed if we do not give it our full individual support? Should we not try to do something about it? What we need is a deep inward conviction and an outward proof of it."

Not long thereafter, Captain Dent was piloting another United Air Lines passenger plane, to Los Angeles. When he prepared to land the wheels did not come out. A belly landing was the only course. The runways were cleared and foamed, the plane circled in the air in order to use up as much fuel as possible, fire engines and ambulances were ready on the ground. While thousands of Americans watched the event on television, Captain Dent brought down his plane impeccably. He was rewarded not only by the gratitude and applause of his passengers but also by a sum of five thousand dollars from his airline. He saw in this sum a little hint from heaven and decided to found with his friend Captain Munger an association aimed at enlisting the support of the American people for the UN. The outward sign of the association was the UN emblem surrounded by the words: "UN We Believe." Dag Hammarskjöld gave it his personal approval.

The first efforts of the organization were directed at pilots and airline personnel who, in the view of the two men, had a particular stake in world peace and order. Later, UN We Believe took on the more ambitious task of building a better understanding for the United Nations among American business and labor circles.[1]

I have often met Captains Dent and Munger, when they pay a quick visit to the United Nations between flights, and I will always remember the happy face of Captain Dent when he told me the story of UN We Believe. He considers his five-thousand-dollar donation to be the best investment he has ever made in his life.

The work of UN We Believe is truly admirable: Due to its efforts, information about the work of the UN and its specialized agencies is

---

[1]As of 2005, UN We Believe is still in existence as the Business Council for the UN (BCUN) of the United Nations Association (UNA).

being conveyed to hundreds of magazines and internal journals of most major firms and labor unions in the United States, thus reaching millions of American workers and employees. The editors of these magazines are brought together each year at the United Nations for a briefing on the state of the world and of international co-operation. TV networks and major advertising firms are voluntarily helping UN We Believe. Throughout the year business luncheons are organized at the UN between presidents of the largest American corporations and UN officials and ambassadors. At these luncheons, stewardesses from American Airlines are present to symbolize the origin of the association. Many other activities of UN We Believe culminate in a yearly ambassadors' dinner shortly before the opening of the General Assembly, at which prominent American businessmen from all over the United States meet with the UN ambassadors and hear famous speakers on world affairs.

I have often addressed UN We Believe groups and accompanied the president of the association, Roger Enloe, or his assistant, John Bryan, on their visits to business communities in various parts of their beautiful country. If my spirit for international co-operation should ever falter, the mere thought of Captains Dent and Munger and their associates would be enough to renew my belief in the United Nations and my determination never to give up.

In a display window of the Biltmore Hotel, on Vanderbilt Avenue in New York, passersby are reminded of the faith in the UN of the two American pilots. Whenever I walk in front of it and see the large UN We Believe poster, I cannot help feeling that the wheels of Captain Dent's DC-7, which refused to unlock over Los Angeles, were in reality turning for peace and a better understanding of all peoples. The world might not be quite the same if the pilot had not asked himself this question: "What is each one of us doing for peace? What can I do for peace?" May his example be followed by many other men and women of good will. The world is in dire need of UN We Believe, UN We Listen, and UN We Act associations.

Never on Tuesday

A little superstition does not hurt.

In August 1975, 180 U.S. astronomers signed a declaration stating that astrology was a fraud devoid of all rational and scientific basis. These learned men were probably right, but nevertheless one may ask oneself why astrology has survived so successfully throughout the ages and is stronger today than ever before, according to the same concerned astronomers. There must be a good reason. Sociologists and psychologists could render us a service by finding the cause of the persistency of astrology and superstition. Personally, I can see two reasons: first, superstition may have beneficial effects on the daily lives of people. Horoscopes and omens are either good or bad: If they are good, the individual, without necessarily believing in them, feels better; if they are bad, he will be more careful and is reminded that accidents and adversity can happen. He thus gains in wisdom and in good behavior. As a matter of fact, curiosity about one's fate is so strong that one may ask how many people, including the 180 astronomers, would resist opening a Chinese fortune cookie and reading its little message!

Second, there seems to be in most of us a well-preserved little corner of belief in the unexplained and the marvelous. This has gained strength as the times became more rational, scientific, and materialistic. There is an instinctive individual rebellion against the idea that everything can be explained in logical, causal, scientific terms. This is a rather reassuring sign of sanity, a robust reminder that total knowledge and understanding will forever escape man, that many mysteries will never yield to our efforts at explanation, however herculean these may be, and that there may be immense mysterious forces in the universe of which we are prisoners and that we will never compre hend.

In my own life, I have come to place particular trust in people who have maintained some belief in superstition and respect for the unknown. They seemed to profess sounder judgment than purely rational and usually harder people. They were more open to the basic, unexplainable streams of life, rather than being locked up in blind self-confidence, as if everything could be unraveled, conquered, or bought. They were also usually kinder people.

One of the most pleasant surprises during my United Nations career was to discover that such attitudes prevailed even among some of the highest UN officials, starting with U Thant himself, who believed that all sentient beings were "struggling in a dark ignorance that blinds them to the truth of their nature and the laws that govern their existence." He had his horoscope read often by his Burmese wife. The following anecdote is another example.

In January 1970 — I was then director of the Budget Division — a close collaborator of U Thant sounded me out as to whether I would like to join his immediate staff. The idea appealed to me immensely, for I had always dreamed that someday I could work directly with a Secretary General and observe the functioning of the organization from the vantage point of this central office. I acquiesced therefore immediately. One condition was put to me: U Thant expected me to act strictly as an international civil servant, devoted exclusively to him and to the organization. This did not pose any problems for me, since such behavior had been my iron rule from the moment I joined the United Nations.

Consultations took place among various officials regarding the date of my transfer and my replacement. Late one Friday afternoon, Mr. Narasimhan, U Thant's Indian Chef de Cabinet, the man under whom I was to serve, called me to his office and said:

"If all goes well and if I am able to complete my consultations quickly, your appointment will be announced on Monday. If not, U Thant will do it on Wednesday."

I could not help noticing the jump from Monday to Wednesday and asked:

"Will U Thant or you be away on Tuesday?"

"No. Why?"

"Because I notice that you have excluded Tuesday as a possibility."

He looked at me seriously and answered:

"My dear Robert, as you may well imagine, your appointment is a very important one, for yourself, for the Secretary General, and for me. I could not visualize for a moment that the risk of such a decision or announcement could be taken on a Tuesday, which is considered an unpropitious day in our countries."

I left his office somewhat puzzled, but smiling inside of me, for I had not expected to find superstition on the thirty-eighth floor of the United Nations.[1] I considered it a good omen for the world that people like U Thant and his Chef de Cabinet were faithful to the beliefs of their forefathers.

There was a statue of Buddha in U Thant's office, a bronze of Shiva in Mr. Narasimhan's, a crucifix by Mazzone in my own, and a little superstition in all our hearts. One common bond was uniting us: a deep commitment to peace, goodness, justice, understanding, and human brotherhood on this planet. To fight for such objectives in our hard and complex world requires indeed a good dose of faith and superstition!

My appointment took place on a Wednesday, and Mr. Narasimhan must have been well advised, for I derived from my years of collaboration with him and with the Secretary General the greatest satisfactions a man can hope for in his life.

It is also noteworthy that the United Nations receives many messages from astrologers and groups of people who believe that earthly events are shaped by astral circumstances. During the past few years many such communications point to an impending era of world

---

[1]The offices of the Secretary General and of his immediate staff are located on the thirty-eighth floor of the UN Secretariat building. Hence the generic term "thirty-eighth floor" given to this group of people.

peace, enlightenment, and human brotherhood, which will apparently be brought about by our entry into the sign of Aquarius.[2] The existence and growth of the United Nations is seen by these people as one of the first signs of this coming age. May these kind astrologers be right and may we all work hand in hand for the fulfillment of their prediction.

[2]Not only astrologers but also serious philosophers believe in the dawning of the Age of Aquarius: see *Carl Jung, Memories, Dreams, Reflections* (New York: Vintage Books, 1961) and Erich Jantsch, "The Quest for Absolute Values," Unified World (Jan.–Mar. 1977).

A Biological View of Mankind

We are witnessing a very unique moment of evolution: the birth of collective organs for the human species.

I receive all kinds of epithets in the United Nations: naive, a nonrealist, a dreamer, a visionary, an idealist, a preacher, a world server, an incurable optimist. The only appellation I don't like is that of a "thinker," for I consider thinking to be an improper way of getting the right answers to the fundamental questions of life. I distrust thought because it involves only part of the human being it excludes in particular the heart; because it is an "effort"; and because my brain is only an infinitesimal and negligible chip of the total mind of mankind. Who am I indeed to dare think out solutions for all humanity? I admire philosophers, ideologists, social reformers, and political thinkers who can sit at their desks and elaborate universal systems, explanations, or schemes for the entire human race. How courageous they are!

I believe instead in life as the best teacher. It has been wonderful to me. It has given me some of the most luminous answers to the great mysteries and complexities of life and of the surrounding world. These answers came rather late and were preceded by many years of learning and observation, especially in the United Nations, that first global watchtower of our planet. They came as enlightenments to questions put to me by others who were curious to know how a man like me felt about some of the fundamental problems of our time. When Fate addresses me a request to speak, I always accept, for it reflects a basic interrogation by human brothers or sisters. I never "think" about the subject and never prepare a written speech. I let the question rest in my mind, I keep it warm and alive, I fall in love with it until the moment when my perception presents itself like a flower opening to the warmth and brilliance of the sun. Lessons from others, questions by others, the vagaries and accidents of life, the fortuity of human encounters and love, those were my real teachers. The greatest blessing by Dame Fate was, of course, to place me at the center of world affairs whence I could observe humanity and the globe at the precise moment when the human race was becoming one, the world global, nations interdependent, the people knowledgeable of each other, and our planet visible from outer space as a self-contained tiny spaceship in the universe.

Yes, I have observed the world with utmost passion, almost ecstasy, for it was a very unique moment in evolution. I would not have dared to present my views in a systematic fashion or to write a book about the United Nations, as so many people do after having attended a few sessions. This adventure was too beautiful, too majestic to be arrogantly forced into a contrived system of thinking. Enlightenment had to come "naturally," at its right moment. A correct idea, view, perception, or truth must grow and mature like the seeds of a plant, like a child in a womb. It must be nourished, cared for, and loved, but it cannot be pushed.

I will never forget the first instance of such an enlightenment. The United Nations had been invited to send a speaker on current political and socio-economic trends and biological evolution to a meeting of the American Institute of Biological Sciences at Amherst University. I decided to go myself, fascinated as I was by the subject and by the participants: anthropologists, artists, biologists, men of religion, etc. I was not disappointed, for the speakers held some very deep perceptions of human evolution as seen from the point of view of their respective disciplines. The religious men spoke of the "sanctity of life" and of their reluctance to compromise with new concepts of birth control and abortion. The biologists held diversity as the supreme law of evolution. The artists spoke about human perceptions, the functioning of the senses and of the brain, and of the meaning of art in recent times. The anthropologists gave their latest views on the origin of man and the causes of the extraordinary growth of the human brain at one stage of evolution.

It was the very day on which the heads of state of the U.S.A. and the U.S.S.R. were meeting in Washington and when East Germany and West Germany were admitted to the United Nations. It was the week during which three men returned to earth after having spent weeks in a sky laboratory.[1] As I listened to the speakers, I suddenly realized that perhaps the adventure of human co-operation in the United Nations was also a great biological event. When my turn came to speak, I placed myself in the frame of mind of biologists and presented to them the work of the United Nations as a living part of an evolutionary process. Here are the main points of what I said:

In the last few years, superimposed on a variety of racial, cultural, political, social, and economic diversities, the world has witnessed the forceful emergence of the oneness of mankind. This concept has long been known to biologists, philosophers, and religious leaders, but only recently did it burst through the crust of national thinking and policies. This result was due to the fantastic advances in science and technology which, since World War II, have reached from the atom and the cell to outer space and to our moon and solar system. It was not the fruit of wishful or utopian thinking but of very hard facts and common concerns which have suddenly seized the human species and its leaders: the atomic scare, the population scare, the environmental scare, the energy and resources scare, and there will be others. New preoccupations, beliefs, and ideas which were totally unknown not long ago emerge one after the other and occupy the forefront of the news as birth pains of the global age. There has never been any precedent of such a situation in the entire previous evolution of mankind. We are entering a totally new period of history.

Thus we find ourselves on the threshold of a new Copernican revolution of thinking about our planet, its biological and chemical processes, our relations with outer space and our sun, our land masses and oceans, our atmosphere, our companion species on earth, and above all the species of direct

[1]June 1973

concern to us namely, the human one. Political, economic, social, and personal thinking, behavior, and fates will all inexorably be affected by the need to take into full account the collective effects of our actions on the physical and biological patterns which we have inherited in the universe. We are moving fast toward a global view of our planet; the concept of the biosphere is pressing itself forcefully upon us and, as a result, many priorities, rights, ambitions, beliefs, principles, and habits will have to undergo change. This process has already begun under our very eyes, and anyone who does not trace it back to its fundamental causes will neither understand our epoch nor discern the trends of the future. Every scientist and every leader, be he political, economic, social, or religious, must work within this new global concept and contribute to the development of higher levels of human life in the biosphere.

The instruments which will help us better understand our interrelations are being developed as part of the global notion of the human species, which is emerging at this juncture of time. It is definitely my impression, as a practitioner of world affairs, that the human race is slowly but surely taking the form of a collective organism, with common concerns, moods, and relations, shaken once in a while by real biological shudders, which seize the entire body from one end to the other. The great universalists of the past, people like Kant, would be thrilled to live today and to see their vision of mankind as an entity take progressive shape.

I have at least one proof of what I say: It concerns the birth of a brain for this new biological body composed of the entire human race. While there are no cellular particles in the human body that are sufficiently "intelligent" to detect or determine the direction of biological evolution and then change themselves accordingly, such a system is being developed for the human species as a whole. In my view, the United Nations and its specialized agencies, together with the mass media and many international efforts, are becoming this collective brain or macrocephalus of humanity.

All problems and preoccupations concerning our planet are being brought under the pressure of global events to the world organization. There is not a subject on earth, there is not a preoccupation of the human race that is not being registered, studied, and debated in this collective stethoscope of our globe. This goes from the atom and genetic engineering to a legal order for outer space and preserving our environment, our cultural diversity, and the heritage of our past. It reaches from world reporting on birth defects and radioactivity to pressing for better standards of living, longer lives, and attaining mankind's multiple and sometimes conflicting dreams for peace, freedom, equality, order, justice, beauty, and environmental safety.

The subject is too immense, as we live it on a daily basis at the United Nations, to be entered into at any length, but let me illustrate at least how the collective brain functions and how the human species begins to respond to it.

Scientists had been warning about the environment for quite a number of years but they were voices in the desert until 1968, when UNESCO organized the first world scientific conference on the biosphere. This was followed almost immediately by a move on the political front by Sweden in the United Nations to convene a world environmental conference, which was held in 1972 in Stockholm. Well, prior to 1968, you could not find a single ministry or governmental department on this earth dealing with the environment. You could barely find any mention of this subject in the newspapers or in economic textbooks. Today, on the contrary, you can count on one hand the number of countries which do not have a ministry or governmental unit dealing with the environment. University libraries are filling with books on the subject and one cannot open a newspaper without reading about it.

On the practical side, the effects have been far-reaching, for nations, firms, local communities, and, last but not least,

individuals heard the message. A global phenomenon and danger was thus registered in time by the brain, which emitted the
necessary warning to the species and to its political, economic,
and social components and leaders. These have begun to react
in the direction of survival and correction, opening a new
chapter in the era of Copernican thinking regarding our terrestrial affairs.

I will give this other example: In 1966, before the environmental issue arose, global concern about our oceans and
seas, which represent two thirds of our planet's surface, was
expressed by the Secretariat of the United Nations and by a
small country, Malta. We were appalled to discover how little
was being done by the collectivity of nations to better know
these vast masses of our planet, with their enormous potential
of protein, mineral, and energy resources for our rapidly growing human species. A lot has been done since then: The oceans
and seas beyond the limits of national jurisdiction have been
declared a common heritage of mankind, an international
regime is being worked out for the exploitation of the seabeds'
riches, and a great impetus was given to international and
national oceanographic research.

One could write a whole treatise about the birth of this
collective brain and warning system of the human species.
Consisting of sixteen UN specialized agencies and several
major UN programs, it will be further strengthened by direct
contacts between the political world and the academic community through a United Nations University, which is to deal
with the collective frontiers, challenges, and dangers of our
planet.

As a further illustration, let me mention the major world
conferences which are being convened by the United Nations
as part of the brain's efforts: In July will start in Paris at
UNESCO a major scientific conference on the sun in the service of mankind, which will review our current knowledge and
technology on solar energy, the effects of the sun on our habitat, and its relations with plant, animal, and human biology.

Soon thereafter, preparations will start for a world conference on the oceans and seas, which will review practically every subject conceivable concerning our seas and oceans, and establish a legal order for this common heritage of mankind.

Next year, in Bucharest, the first world population conference in the entire history of mankind will be held. A year thereafter, a world conference will gather in Canada on human settlements, a field of vital importance where our projections indicate a staggering urban concentration all around the world with its economic, social, biological, and environmental effects.

Two years later, the United Nations will convene a world water conference to review this most important cycle, which from times immemorial has ignored political borders and human divisions and which is being at long last recognized as one of the binding elements and common concerns of the human species.

New global subjects will come up one after the other. For example, I would not be surprised if, as a result of the dramatic drought in the Sahelian-Sudanese region of Africa and the extension of the Sahara Desert, the African countries were to ask for a world conference on the deserts.[2]

All this forms part of biological evolution. The human species continues to probe out, on ever larger scales, the possibilities and limits of its terrestrial and perhaps tomorrow extraterrestrial habitat. Despite the avalanche of problems, despite the unsolved mysteries, despite the frustrations, inequalities, impatience, and despair, this is one of the most thrilling and challenging periods of our planet's history. There remains so much to be done and I am personally very confident that we will find the necessary adaptations of our brains, appetites, beliefs, feelings, and behavior to find new equilibria and to select what is good for us instead of bad on our small

[2]They requested it indeed for 1977. Two further conferences were held in 1975: a world food conference and a world employment conference. A world conference on science and technology is foreseen for 1979.

spaceship Earth circling in the universe, surrounded by its thin but so fantastically rich biosphere of only a few miles, containing all life of our solar system. ...

When I finished, Dr. Ernst Mayer, a famous anthropologist from the University of Chicago, reputed for his work on the evolution of the human brain, had the following comment:

"This comes as a total surprise to me. I have never heard the work of the UN presented in this way. I felt as if I were witnessing a rare moment in evolution — namely, the birth of a collective organ to a species, a moment similar to that when the first protozoa developed into a metazoa. Perhaps indeed, the human race is entering a new period of evolution, a period of global life, an event that will only be fully understood by future generations."

I have never forgotten these words, which were very precious to me, for I often heard later the evolution of mankind detracted with various comments, such as these:

"The fate of the human species will be that of a school of fishes overpopulating a pond. At one point, the fishes become too numerous, they overstress their ecological environment, and they all perish. This is what will happen to humanity too." Or, "When apes get too numerous and live in overcrowded conditions, they become aggressive and kill each other. The same will happen to men overpopulating this planet. Humans will destroy each other through crime and war."

Thenceforth, I was able to answer:

"Nothing of the sort is likely ever to happen, for there is a fundamental difference between fishes and apes, and mankind: The human species has a vastly superior brain and communications system. It is quite capable, through a multiplicity of efforts and organs developed of late, to better know and probe its planet, diagnose new perils, give the necessary warnings, and act in common. There is little danger of a collective self-destruction through human proliferation and misbehavior. On the contrary, I believe that, for the first time ever, humanity will be able to organize paradise on earth."

The biologists' meeting at Amherst was my first enlightenment that something important was happening in the world. It was not the result of chance or accident, but conformed to a basic biological pattern. An extraordinarily complex, highly developed species, the human race, superior to all others in its capacity to understand, dominate, and change the surrounding world, was trying to live the longest and fullest possible lives, to survive successfully in unprecedented numbers, and to reach full consciousness of its existence on little planet Earth and of its cosmic presence in the universe.

I felt so happy because I was allowed to live this prodigious adventure and to bring my little contribution to it. What a distance Fate had allowed me to cover since I left my little town on the border between France and Germany with its horizon of wars, uniforms, tombs, and quarreling nations. If only each human could feel the same elation at seeing humanity at long last proceed toward world oneness and harmony. So I gallantly finished my speech as follows:

"These are facts of very profound significance for our future progress and survival, and there is one conclusion that I dare to place before you: There will never be again any world war. Humanity has entered its global age with a narrow escape from a world holocaust, but we are over the hump, and the worst is past in this regard."

As I complete this manuscript in 1977, I notice that, for several months now, there has been no active conflict anywhere. Perhaps this is the beginning of a new era. If such peace can be maintained year after year, thanks to the restraint and vigilance of every nation, perhaps the day will also dawn in the not too distant future when real disarmament will become a possibility. I am certain of it, I can feel it with all my soul: The world is entering a period of lasting peace and co-operation. It cannot be otherwise. It must not be otherwise.

A Moral and Spiritual Dimension

Humanity must now transcend itself into the moral and spiritual spheres.

After so many years of trial and error, the pattern of the prodigious human march toward greater fulfillment and consciousness is now becoming clear: For the first time in evolution, mankind is emerging as a true global entity, with a bloodstream, a nervous system, a heart, a brain, and a sense of common destiny. Human unity is no longer a dream of the philosophers, humanists, and prophets. It has entered the arena of public debate. In less than three decades, after millions of years of painful evolution, humanity is now being forged into a unit above and beyond all separate partial units. For the first time ever, potent common human interests, menaces, and hopes are finding their expression in worldwide institutions.

Second, human concerns and consciousness today are all-encompassing: They reach from the stars to the atom, from outer space to the core of the earth, from the atmosphere to the abyss of the seas, from food to microbiology, from world population to individual human rights. This is the product of a multitude of dreams and efforts of innumerable individuals and institutions. Within a short thirty years we have witnessed the most incredible explosion of knowledge and concern radiating far into the universe and the infinitely small. What incredible progress, what gigantic steps have been accomplished! The brain of mankind is penetrating everything everywhere. We have been given a Copernican overview, a magnificently clear framework, the skeleton of total understanding of our place and destiny in space and in evolution. And we will now make further progress in unlocking the secrets of the functioning of the human being and of humanity's thoughts, sentiments, and consciousness. The great work of art of putting flesh around the skeleton, of giving it beauty and life, is only beginning now. Millions of men and women have the privilege and joy of contributing to the task of perfecting human knowledge on everything in the heavens and on earth. Never have there been so many world scientists, thinkers, seers, and visionaries all concerned with the total state of the world and the plenitude of human life. What an epoch!

Third, mankind's vision is becoming all-inclusive in time. Our view is reaching from the Creation to the Apocalypse. The future of our globe, of its population, resources, food, energy, climate, and environment, the preservation of our past, of our immensely rich capital of cultures, languages, beliefs, animals, plants, and genetic diversity are becoming of concern to everyone: They are in the daily news. This revolution in thinking, this new time dimension of the human mind, this birth of futurology is just another major aspect of the gigantic and rapid march of man toward total consciousness. Discoveries worthy of Galileo are being made by the dozens every year.

There is still one major feature missing in this grandiose view dawning upon the world. U Thant knew it when he said that a moral and spiritual dimension was needed for our progress. There is already a good deal of morality in international work: We strive toward peace, justice, welfare, human dignity, understanding, help, and human rights. But there is also a prodigious lot of immorality: armaments, protracted conflicts, excessive wealth alongside hunger and despair, numerous violations of the UN Charter and of basic human rights. Also, what have such moral concepts as "truthfulness," "love," "compassion," "understanding," and "kindness" to do in an organization that reflects above all the hard realities and interests of our time, the struggle for "more" by everybody? As for spirituality, one cannot see it anywhere, except for its incarnations in Dag Hammarskjöld and in a wonderful kind-hearted son of Asia, U Thant.

I was at a loss, when in October 1975, on the occasion of the thirtieth anniversary of the United Nations, I was invited to a gathering of spiritual leaders in New York City. The meetings took place in the Cathedral of St. John the Divine. They were interspersed with various religious rites. Most impressive was the final ceremony, held in the Dag Hammarskjöld Auditorium of the United Nations. Leaders from the Hindu, Buddhist, Christian, Moslem, and Jewish faiths were assembled. Also seated on the podium was a 104-year-old American Indian chief. A tall, strong young Indian was standing behind him, holding hands on his shoulders in order to let his strength flow into the old man. Lady Srimata Gayatri Devi of the Hindu faith spoke first. She referred to the work of the philosopher Ramakrishna, who had studied the world's main religions and had concluded that they all shared the same objectives. She spoke of the world's seers, prophets, and visionaries who had been illumined by great unifying principles: spirituality, ethics, God, the presence of all in one and of one in all, the union between the inner self and world consciousness. The speakers for Buddhism, Islam, and Judaism held similar beliefs. All shared their prophets' beliefs in the oneness of mankind and all nations under one God or unifying principle. At the end of the ceremony, Mother Teresa of Calcutta took the floor. She used very sparse and simple words. She spoke in the name of all the poor, the unloved, and the unwanted in the world, including those in our own homes. She stressed the need of all humans to be somebody to someone else, reminding me very much of Abbé Pierre. She said:

"The poor are brothers and sisters in the same family, created by the same loving God. If you do not know them, you do not love them, and you do not serve them. . . . We must love until it hurts, especially in these great United Nations."

She told the audience how she had picked up recently a dying woman in the streets of Calcutta and had cared for her in her dispensary.

"She was going to die. She took my hand and said to me: 'Thank you.' I received infinitely more from her than what I had given." Mother Teresa's moving simplicity brought tears to my eyes. She too had found a great unifying principle: the principle of love, of love until it hurts.

The extraordinary ceremony ended with a meditation under the guidance of a Benedictine monk. Seldom had I seen such profound oneness in spirit, such vibrating understanding and warm brotherhood under the roof of the United Nations. The event was one of the most beautiful tributes the United Nations received on its thirtieth anniversary.

It was a revelation to me. I suddenly realized that the Hindu philosophy, the Koran, the Talmud, the Bible, the American Indians' worship for nature, Mother Teresa's poignant love, U Thant's Buddhism without God, Pope John's encyclical *Pacem in Terris*, Pope Paul's visit and message to the United Nations, etc., had all the same meaning: They were multiple manifestations of man's eternal quest for a moral and spiritual order on this planet, for the attainment of the highest form of life, for the fullest possible human consciousness of all. These spiritual leaders had come to the UN because they felt that the UN was repeating all over, on a universal and nontheological basis, the same old human story and dream. Their message was the same as that of U Thant: Humanity needs to transcend itself into a moral and spiritual plane and to open its doors to love, understanding, brotherhood, self-restraint, and morality. It had to ask itself the ultimate cosmic questions: Why are we on earth? What is the meaning of life? What are our deeper, true relations with the surrounding world and with the universe?

Yes, this was the last, great panel still missing in the grandiose fresco of humanity's extraordinary ascent: the tremendous material and intellectual breakthroughs of the past three hundred years had to culminate in a moral and spiritual dimension. It was inexorable. Humanity's progress in the physical and intellectual spheres could not be the end. A similar advance was now needed in the moral and spiritual fields. The human species was entering into an entirely new phase of evolution. We would now witness also the expansion of the heart and of the soul of mankind.

Yes, it was ineluctable. For the first time in history, in the great global grip that had seized humanity, believers and nonbelievers, theists and atheists were all striving toward the same objective: a peaceful, just, and happy life for all. Great past visions — religious, philosophical, humanistic, and others — had all had the same total concept of humanity, the same Copernican view from the infinitely large to the infinitely small, the same time dimension from the Creation to the Apocalypse, the same total perception of the physical, mental, moral, and spiritual nature of man. But all former beliefs had had their origin in a particular region or culture or with individual prophets, visionaries, or schools of thought. This led to endless con flicts and wars among the tenants of universal truth. Today the story is being repeated worldwide with the participation of all peoples, dreams, thoughts, and perceptions extant, and on the basis of hitherto unavailable global files.

Yes, the UN is repeating the same old story all over again, but on an unprecedented planetary and evolutionary scale, within a total time frame, and with a final great thrust toward a total comprehension and ultimate fulfillment of the prodigy of life.

Morality is simply the expression of the highest interest of the group — this time of the entire humanity living in a limited biosphere. Spirituality is the perennial search for total consciousness and union with the cosmos, the infinitely large, the outer reaches of the heavens, the conjunction of inner and outer space.

Despite the insane armaments race, the persisting horrid world injustices, and the breaches of fundamental human rights, despite all the colossal errors and blindness of the leaders, the wealthy, and the powerful, a great tranquil evolution has seized humanity and our planet in its grips. Soon there will be no longer any absolute powers. No one will rule the world, and everybody will be ruled by the world. Increasingly, the doings and freedoms of peoples, firms, institutions, and governments will be dictated by the laws of survival on this planet, by the constraints and limitations of our magnificently rich but so fragile and thin biosphere.

It had taken millions of years to come to this point. It had been a bumpy and winding road to discover what held the heavens and earth together. The world had deviated from the enlightenment of its early prophets. It had erred, blinded by the success of science and mind, oblivious of the power of the heart and soul. But now one could see the glorious old story repeated by and for the entire humanity, above, beyond, and including all dreams, religions, Gods, beliefs, systems, and ideologies. A transcended human consciousness was knocking at the doors of mankind's first global institutions. A moral and spiritual or cosmic dimension would soon be added to the United Nations. I had the privilege of living right in the middle of one of the most unique adventures in the entire evolution of the human race.

As a tribute to this memorable day, I see it fitting to reproduce here the meditation conducted in the Dag Hammarskjöld Auditorium and the text of the spiritual declaration adopted by the conference.

Meditation on the United Nations

Brother Steindl-Rast

Sisters and Brothers in the Spirit.

We have been witnesses of an important and deeply moving event, important not only for us who witnessed it, but also for the history of the United Nations and so for the whole human family.

It is only fitting that we should want to celebrate the closing of this great event by a grateful gesture of the heart.

But it would not be enough if someone pronounced a blessing or prayer in front of you. We must make this grateful gesture of the heart together at this moment. I invite you to do this.

Since we are truly one in heart, we ought to be able to find a common expression of the Spirit who moves us at this moment. But the diversity of our languages tends to divide us. Yet, where the language of words fails, the silent language of gestures helps to express our unity. Using this language, then

Let us rise and stand.

Let our rising be the expression that we are rising to this occasion in deep mindfulness of what it signifies.

Let our standing be a mindful gesture: mindful of the ground on which we are standing, the one little plot of land on this earth not belonging to *one* nation, but to all nations united. It is a very small piece of land, indeed, but it is a symbol of human concord, a symbol of the truth that this poor, mistreated earth belongs to all of us together.

As we stand, then, like plants standing on a good plot of ground, let us sink our roots deep into our hidden unity. Allow yourself to feel what it means to stand and to extend your inner roots.

Rooted in the soil of the heart, let us expose ourselves to the wind of the Spirit, the one Spirit who moves all who let themselves be moved. Let us breathe deeply the breath of the One Spirit.

Let our standing bear witness that we take a stand on common ground.

Let our standing be an expression of reverence for all those who before us have taken a stand for human unity.

Let us stand with reverence on the ground of our common human endeavor, joining all those who stood on this ground, from the first shaper of tools to the engineers of the most complex machines and institutions.

Let us stand with reverence on the common ground of the human quest for meaning, side by side with all who ever stood on this ground in their searching thought, in their celebration of beauty, in their dedicated service.

Let us stand in reverence before all those who on our common ground stood up to be counted, stood up — and were cut down.

Let us remember that to stand up as we have now stood up implies a readiness to lay down one's life for that for which one stands.

Let us stand in awe before those thousands upon thousands — known and unknown — who have laid down their lives for the common cause of our human family.

Let us bow our heads. Let us bow our heads to them.

Let us stand and bow our heads, because we stand under judgment.

We stand under judgment, for "One is the human Spirit." If we are one with the heroes and prophets, we are also one with those who persecuted and killed them. One with the henchmen as we are one with the victims. We all share the glory of human greatness and the shame of human failure.

Allow me to invite you now to focus your mind on the most inhuman act of destruction you can find in your memory. And now take this, together with all human violence, all human greed, injustice, stupidity, hypocrisy, all human misery, and lift it all up, with all the strength of your heart, into the stream of compassion and healing that pulsates through the heart of the world — that center in which all our hearts are one. This is not an easy gesture. It may almost seem too difficult for some of us. But until we can reach and tap with our deepest roots this common source of concord and compassion, we have not yet claimed within our own hearts that oneness that is our common human birthright.

Standing firm, then, in this oneness, let us close our eyes.

Let us close our eyes to bring home to ourselves our blindness as we face the future.

Let us close our eyes to focus our minds on the inner light, our one common light, in whose brightness we shall be able to walk together even in the dark.

Let us close our eyes as a gesture of trust in the guidance of the one Spirit who will move us if we open our hearts.

"One is the human Spirit," but the human Spirit is more than human, because the human heart is unfathomable.

Into this depth let us silently sink our roots. There lies our only source of peace.

In a moment, when I will invite you to open again your eyes, I will invite you also to turn in this Spirit to the person next to you with a greeting of peace. Let our celebration culminate and conclude in this gesture, by which we will send one another forth as messengers of peace. Let us do this now.

Peace be with you all!

Statement of Spiritual Leaders:
Read at the United Nations
on October 24, 1975

We, the delegates to the conference "One Is the Human Spirit," who met in New York City from the nineteenth to the twenty-fourth of October 1975 on the occasion of the thirtieth anniversary of the United Nations, affirm the following:

Humanity's extraordinary achievements in the scientific, technical, and economic fields during the past thirty years have led to a greater physical and psychological unity and interdependence of all peoples of the world. This unity must now be translated into the social and moral spheres if further progress is to be made toward permanent peace, greater justice, and human brotherhood.

Paramount to this unity is the utilization of the spiritual resources that are inherent in the religious traditions of mankind. The horrors of current and possible future wars, the destruction of the earth through the abuses of technology, and the vastness of problems confronting the human condition require the rededication of all peoples, in an awakened sense of the unity of the human spirit, to enhanced co-operation toward the building of a peaceful and just world.

In all cultures and in all ages, the spiritual vision found at the core of the world's religions is one that encompasses the wholeness of life, which is beyond any divisions, whether political, religious, or ideological. However, the religions themselves have too often violated the principle of sharing and co-operation and have become critical causes of misunderstanding, separation, and active hostility.

But the crises of our time are challenging the world religions to release a new spiritual force transcending religious, cultural, and national boundaries into a new consciousness of the oneness of the human community and so putting into effect a spiritual dynamic toward the solutions of world problems. This quickening spirit seen, for instance, in ecumenical events, such as Vatican Council II and the World Fellowship of Buddhists, is rising in our midst as a powerful operation of Spirit in history. We affirm a new spirituality, divested of insularity and directed toward a planetary consciousness.

In the light of this awareness, we affirm that humanity's future must rest on a spiritually based ethics in which individuals, groups, and institutions will find the creative wisdom to direct their behavior and a profound sensibility for what is good and bad in the human community.

The present state of worldwide anxiety, which is characteristic of all great periods of radical transition, must give way to an expression of dynamic hope and faith in the capacity of mankind, especially its youth, to build a new earth, a more humane community, a future open to greater joy and more creative becoming.

The great religious and spiritual movements of our time stand ready to unite around their common spiritual and moral vision and to contribute to the development of a morality and ethics that is mindful of and actively concerned with basic human rights and freedoms, the natural world and our shared environment, and the vital need for world peace. Recognizing the importance and value of every spiritual tradition, we especially seek religious freedom for people of all religions, not only major religions, but also every other faith in which men believe, whether in Europe or Asia, North America or South America, Africa, Australia, or Oceania. It is crucial at this time to listen to those traditions that possess a deep bond and communion with nature and that foster a sacred and harmonious relation between man and earth. Religious traditions offer a rich reservoir of practical wisdom for the development and unfolding of the many potentials of the human being. These resources should be brought to bear fully in the world's search for a better future.

The United Nations deserves high praise for its remarkable efforts and contributions to the advancement of peace, understanding, non-recourse to violence, international co-operation, greater equity, economic development, racial equality, a better environment and quality of life, and the harmonization of the actions of nations during some of the most difficult and dangerous thirty years of human history. Nevertheless, the tasks remain immense, and insufficient progress has been made by the United Nations on some of the major issues of our time — in particular, disarmament, economic development, and human rights.

In light of the dangers and crises that so clearly lie ahead of us, we call on all leaders of every ideology and on the member delegates of the United Nations to extend their vision and concern to the entire globe and to all its inhabitants, and to bring co-operation through the United Nations to ever higher levels so as to achieve fully the noble goals and words of the Charter, in particular, "to save future generations from the scourge of war . . . , and to reaffirm faith in fundamental human rights, in the dignity and worth of the human person, in the equal rights of men and women and of nations large and small, and to establish conditions under which justice and respect for the obligations arising from treaties and other sources of international law can be maintained, and to promote social progress and better standards of life in larger freedom."

In conclusion, the delegates of the conference "One Is the Human Spirit" propose that the time is ripe for the religions of the world to bring together in concert their several visions in aid of the United Nations in its endeavor to build a better human society. To this end, we strongly recommend that the United Nations consider the creation of an agency that will bring the much-needed resources and inspirations of the spiritual traditions to the solution of world problems.

Epilogue

Love for life is the fundamental ingredient of all recipes for happiness.

It was a sunny, magnificent spring morning. I was walking to my beloved little railroad station of Ardsley-on-Hudson. My heart was filled with happiness and my eyes were feasting on the wonders and beauties of nature unfolding along my path. But this calm symphony with the surrounding world was suddenly cut short when I remembered the sad words uttered by a friend of mine the day before:

"My marriage is broken. For some reason that she still has to explain to me, my wife has 'decided' not to love me anymore. All is finished. I feel like gliding into an abyss. You would not believe how everything has changed in my family from one day to another. It is almost unbearable. It is like hell on earth."

And he described to me how in the same little human group he was shepherding, happiness had given way to bitterness, understanding to conflict, trust to suspicion, unity to discord, co-operation to obstruction, thoughtfulness to hostility.

As I continued to walk, gradually oblivious of the surrounding world, I thought that my friend's comments were applicable to the entire human family. I knew it from my work at the UN, where I observed that so many international conflicts arose from a primary decision to hate, belittle, or subjugate another nation, culture, race, ideology, or system. But here, in the midst of nature, I suddenly realized that it was an even more universal law valid for all relations between man and the external world. I resolved to make a test:

Like my friend's wife, I "decided" to stop loving nature and to dislike it instead. Forthwith, the beautiful Hudson River became an unnecessary, ugly mass of wasteful water, eternally and boringly renewed for no intelligible purpose. The trees turned into senseless, grotesque parasols fighting in the air with their leaves for a little solar energy and in the ground with their roots for some moisture and chemical nutrients, again for no recognizable purpose. The flowers seemed vain, the crows were killers, the squirrels were vicious, my dreams were illusions, my joy was childish, my job was senseless, my entire life was a wastebasket filled with despair, hopelessness, and death at the end. The more I let the wheels of this new mood unravel its abyss of mud, the more darkness, pestilence, and venom upwelled. I soon felt like vomiting at life, and it suddenly struck me how easy it was to call forth the specter of suicide. I stopped quickly, awed by the forces I had unleashed in myself.

Emerging from this dreadful experience and shaking off its last ugly images, I found myself once more confirmed in my old, intuitive belief, which had guided me all my life — namely, that only one recipe can solve man's problems on his little planet and perhaps on other planets as well: the indomitable will for life, the law of voluntary, determined, conscious love for life and for the world.

Yes, in war and in peace, in youth and in old age, in opulence and in poverty, in liberty and in prison, in health and in sickness, in activity and in leisure, in success and in failure, in city and in country, in company and in solitude, in the immense maze of human relations there is only one great recipe conducive to happiness: love.

I have kept this word for the end, like a cook who reserves his preferred recipe to crown his previous work. To prove that love is the way out of all suffering and the key to happiness, let me briefly recapitulate what a person can "rationally" expect from life:

- Man is a tiny speck of dust lost in the vast universe on a minuscule planet hanging and twirling around a half-extinct sun, in one of the far and deserted corners of the Milky Way, one of many billions of galaxies.

- On this planet, an individual person is one of four billion peo
  ple squeezed on a few land masses in a fragile and thin biosphere only a few miles thick.

- Man, even at the highest peak of his earthly glory, is strictly
  nothing. Alexander, Caesar, Napoleon, Shakespeare, Leonardo,
  Goethe, Buddha, Confucius, Churchill, De Gaulle, and even
  my dear U Thant are echoless names only a few miles away
  from our planet. So are those of the richest, most powerful,
  most inventive, most productive, most admired, and most
  publicized people on earth. Man is a lost, anonymous prisoner
  in a colony of human bacteria roaming about on a drop of
  unstable mud in fathomless space.

- All life in the end takes a turn for the worse; it finishes in death
  on a time scale that defies human imagination. Someday our
  planet will explode and vanish again into the universe. Every
  cell of our body, every rock on our planet has at one point been
  part of another star and will someday be part of another star.
  Our prestigious solar system is only a minute happening in the
  life of billions of fellow stars. On the time scale of eternity, of a
  galaxy, of a sun, of a planet, the longest life of any person on
  earth is tantamount to nothing. My dear parents have died
  only a few years ago and already their memory is lost forever.

- Most of this precious, infinitesimal span of life is wasted: a
  blind infancy, years of studies and training, military service,
  specialization, work, worries, the building of a nest for a family, the search for security, a third of the time lost in sleep, and
  before we know it, old age is upon us, with its string of miseries, maladies, impotencies, and deaths. Every minute one
  hundred people die on this planet, and yet the globe continues
  to spin unperturbed on its multibillion-year-long journey.

- And what is this beautiful human society into which we are
  born? A values game, a profit game, a collection of endless
  interest groups soliciting people to join and to fight for any
  conceivable cause, be it a nation, a race, an ideology, a belief, an

institution, a company, a product, or an employer. And in this process we lose most of our life in conflict, competition, lies, false values, distortions, jealousies, trifles, and dissatisfactions, often forgetting that the only worthwhile "institutions" on this planet are the individual, his family, and the family of all peoples.

Vanitas vanitatum, omnia vanitas (Everything is vain, hopeless, senseless). The worm feeds on bacteria, the little bird eats the worm, the crow eats the bird, and the crow is eaten by bacteria. And not a single living being, including man, is better off on this wretched planet of ours. All is death, destruction, war of the species, biophagy, eating up each other in order to live.

One could unfold this gloomy picture forever: life reduced to chemical reactions or energy transfers under the orchestration of the sun's hydrogen explosions; man a prisoner of an oxygen cycle, a nitrogen cycle, a carbon cycle, a water cycle; the likelihood of new ice ages and geological upheavals; the instability of the earth's crust; the diminishing of its rotation; the depletion of good air and water; the limits of growth, wealth, and life; the atomic menaces on the biosphere; the proliferation of armaments; the extreme injustices in the world; humans dying of hunger and others suffocating in their fat; beggars in the streets and millionaires in their skyscrapers deciding what people will eat, drink, wear, read, and think; innumerable beings killed in the wombs of their mothers and in atrocious homicidal wars; endless violations of freedom and of human rights; vital resources squandered on waste amid want and misery, etc.

To see anything admirable in such a society and on such a planet seems tantamount to madness.

And yet . . .

And yet . . .

And yet . . . man cannot accept the above premises as the bases for his earthly sojourn. If he did, life would be meaningless, and suicide would be the only way out. Indeed, many of these hopeless facets are heralded by the pessimists as proofs of their philosophical outlook. But man has also the admirable faculty to see everything from a positive, affirmative point of view, from the sunny instead of the somber side of life: he can see a bottle half full or half empty, he can recognize most lucidly the above conditions and reject them almost immediately as being death blows to the only asset he possesses: life. He can see good instead of bad and look at himself as an unmatched miracle in the universe, never to be repeated again. He can see his life as almost an eternity when compared with the infinitesimal life span of an atomic particle. He can see the day instead of the night, light instead of darkness, the glory of the sun instead of hydrogen explosions, the beauty of a being instead of his skull and guts, the construction of peace instead of the horrors of war, the miracle of life instead of decay, the preciousness of a family instead of future tombs, babies born instead of the dead. . . .

The key to such an outlook is love, affirmation of life, thankfulness for life. Some have called it sanctity of life (most religions), reverence for life (the Jains, Albert Schweitzer), celebration of life (Norman Cousins). I prefer to call it passion for life, the key to all, the result of a personal, determined decision. Whatever its name, anyone who receives the gift of life ought to feel fathomlessly indebted to it, for he has been given a unique treasure in the universe. He is a true miracle on a planet that is itself a miracle. He should love life from deep within, whatever others may think or proclaim, despite the wars, the prisons, the injustices, the struggles, the inequalities, the false values, the dogmas, the noises, the ideologies, the jealousies, the fashions, and the contortions of the four billion human fleas jumping around him. I live, therefore I am. Life is all I have. Life is beautiful, divine, miraculous, fathomless. Life is to love, to do, to learn, to think, to imagine, to talk, to receive, to feel, to understand, to mate, to give birth, and to embrace in one's heart and brain the entire creation. Every moment of life is creation. In every human life all can be accomplished. Man can taste totality and eternity. He can penetrate the infinitely small and the infinitely large. There is so much a human can do and experience! The miseries of life are merely specks of dust on a wonderful object of art. Not to revere, not to love, not to wonder, not to be impassioned with the miraculous, brief droplet of life is a crime, a waste, an outrage, and a stupidity. The more I have lived, the more I have concluded that unhappy people are simply unintelligent people.

Merely think of the unborn who will never see a sunrise, hear the song of a bird, know the ecstasy of love, rejoice at the smile of a child, hear the murmur of a brook, feel the warmth of a home. They could rightly turn to the Creator and say:

"Look at this human. He is alive and yet unhappy and complaining unceasingly. Make him die. I am ready to take his place, and I promise you to be always happy and grateful for your gift."

Yes, we must visualize at all times how precious life will seem at the moment of death. Then only will we be ready to give up our pretensions, foolishness, and possessions for a measure of additional life. "All my wealth, all my power for one more year of life."

Love for life, passion for life, deep gratitude for every moment of it, extending one's heart and brain into eternity and totality, from the fishes and the fowl to the stars, from youth to old age, from the glaciers to the tropics, from the prodigy of birth to the mystery of death, man can indeed partake in all creation if he switches on, deep inside, the will for life, the decision for happiness, the option for love. I have "decided" to love my life, to throw in my gauntlet for it, to believe in it, to find it exalting in every respect, at every moment, from the beginning to the end.

There is so much magic in life, in these colors, in these shapes, in this drop of shining light in the gigantic dark universe. Yes, our planet is a prodigious miracle, a unique happening in billions of years of evolution, in aeons of light-years of space. We will never cherish it enough. We will never be grateful enough. This miracle should be the object of our constant love, joy, and admiration. We should stand in awe before the mysterious forces that brought it into being. But instead, so many of us are complaining, unhappy, and somber. How is that possible? Why can't we realize that all this could well not be, that evolution could have produced a different planet, a lifeless planet, at another distance from the sun, with a different inclination or orbit, a different atmosphere, flora, and fauna, another human body, heart, and mind? All great religions, prophets, and visionaries saw it better than the scientists of today. They demanded respect for creation and for the mysterious forces behind it. Our colossal contemporary knowledge should have increased our elation and our thankfulness for the wonders of nature. Instead, we have lost much of our love and happiness. We must lift ourselves again high above our microscopes, telescopes, books, newspapers, and computers, and see again the total beauty of a flower, of a brook, of a woman, of a child, of the world, of the stars. We forgot the secret of secrets, the great divine simplifying principle in ourselves that creates beauty: love. With Pablo Casals we should all exclaim:

"... The child must know that he is a miracle, a miracle, that since the beginning of the world there hasn't been and until the end of the world there will not be another child like him. . . . I am a miracle. I am a miracle like a tree is a miracle, like a flower is a miracle."

Yes, our miraculous planet Earth should irradiate human thankfulness and joy into every direction of the universe.

Love is the only way out, the secret of secrets. Happiness is a state of mind, a click inside us, a conscious, determined decision or will to embrace with fascination, enthusiasm (that is, by God possessed), the entire world and creation. Happiness is total consciousness. Happiness is the peak fulfillment of life. It is a human's own doing, his greatest power and liberty. Happiness is not external to man, it is a genial force in him. It cannot be elsewhere. It is not part of nature or of the world, it is an attribute, an essence of the human person. It is above prison, death, poverty, disability, injustice, age, inequality, and prejudice. A vagabond in a ditch, a deprived artist or poet, an invalid, an uneducated tribesman surrounded by his wife and children can be a thousand times happier than an insatiable neurotic millionaire in his skyscraper. Billions of happy humans have walked on this planet throughout the ages who did not have the blessings of today. Happiness is the great revanche of the poor, the dreamers, the poets, the artists, the visionaries, the simple, the wise, the diminished, and all those guided by the heart rather than by power, money, and interest. Happiness is increasingly vital in a world of growing numbers, complexity, and anonymity, where glory is becoming increasingly difficult.

Happiness is the sole satisfactory answer I have found in the sea of puzzles, questions, mysteries, turmoils, and competing claims in which we bathe. Happiness against and despite everything, at all ages and in all conditions, is a great act of freedom, a refusal to postpone life on the pretext that someday conditions will improve, that the world will be better, that a new system or leader will solve everything, that society will be reformed, that war, revolution, or evolution will generate justice and paradise on earth, that my merits will be recognized, etc. I would feel like a fool and hate myself today if I had foregone my happiness and waited for the fulfillment of such empty promises. Happiness and enjoyment of life are the highest expressions of individual intelligence, liberty, and fulfillment of life. Happiness is likely to be the most important single objective of tomorrow's civilization, when mankind at long last will ask itself again these long-neglected questions: "Why are we on earth? What do we expect from life? How can we maximize these precious years with which we are blessed?" These are the basic questions. And the answers are: to live optimum physical, mental, moral, and spiritual lives, to open oneself to others, to aggrandize ourselves through others, to listen to the great voices of nature and the universe, to perceive the unknown, to live in unison and love with all that is on earth and in the heavens, to pray, to meditate, to know one's inner world, to extend one's heart and mind into the infinite heart and mind of humankind, to live fully and passionately our life, to let the world and the people enter in great wondrous streams, to be thrilled at life, to be part of life, deeply, intensely, consciously, as we are indeed in flesh, in brain, and in feeling. That is love. That is the only worthwhile life and way of helping a new man emerge from evolution. To the philosophers of pessimism and doom I would therefore retort: Happiness in spite of everything, for belief in mankind, love for life and hope in the future are the only avenues to human survival. All the rest is blindness and denial of life. Happiness is triumph of life; pessimism is its defeat.

Someday political leaders too will find again the simple word "happiness" as the ultimate goal of their efforts.[1] Then we will see

---

[1] It is significant that the word "happiness" begins to appear more frequently in the speeches of heads of state and foreign ministers at the United Nations.

again good rulers comparable to the wise kings and emperors of the past who still occupy a cherished place in the memory of men.

Pending that time, even in a world of turmoil and noise, each of us can carry his own shell of joy and dreams, his monastery of silence and thoughts, protected like a duck by his impermeable feathers. Rather than wait for a world of angels, it is in the interest of each of us to define and assert our own happiness. This will spread to others and demonstrate that happiness and serenity are possible even in a world of change and crisis. Such a step would be a most important contribution to the total peace of humankind. As I finish writing this book, I am increasingly discovering a great moral law on this planet — namely, that happiness is a duty of man. The greater his blessings, the greater are his obligations toward life. The best contribution a decently endowed person can make to the purification of the present atmosphere is to proclaim: "I am happy, I am content, I am grateful for all my blessings, I am living a beautiful life. Thank you, O God, for Your miraculous gift. I have so much. I will now work for the happiness of others."

There is a great creative force, a "Pygmalion effect," in human attitudes such as love, altruism, dream, meditation, prayer, autosuggestion, exaltation, belief, idealism, poetry, happiness, and even illusion. Our scientific age has tried to smother and belittle these qualities to hide its incapacity to explain them. But they are here. They have always been here. Since the beginnings of time they were man's principal means of sorting out and surmounting the incredibly complex and inexplicable world surrounding him. Science has not pierced these mysteries. It can dissect and explain the body of a woman, analyze the water of a lake, the air, the atmosphere, the marble of a statue, the color of a flower, the rays of the sun, the stars of the sky, but it cannot explain their beauty and my love for them. To dream, to pray, to meditate, to love, to believe, to be happy, to be a poet, to be an idealist, to paint, to sculpt, to write, to sing are to create and to escape from the dark ignorance surrounding us. None of these qualities will ever be explained by scientists, for they are above measurement and explanation. Scientists depreciate them because these qualities resist scientific investigation. In my stories, selected from a lifelong experience, I tried to show that these attributes have a potent effect and that they may be at the core of humanity's sanity and survival. A dream, a prayer, an ideal, a belief, an autosuggestion, an illusion, a movement of the heart can be very powerful realities indeed. The time has come for the world to transcend itself above the scientific age and re-establish the role of these great old motors of human progress. Perhaps the key to our future lies in a marriage between the rational and the irrational, between science and the special human capacity to create happiness, beauty, and peace by our own volition, with our hearts and minds. A useful role for the scientists would be to study the effects of these properties on the well-being and func-tioning of the human being. Luminous relationships might emerge. In the vast planetary discussion of human fate that takes place today, good attention has been paid to the surrounding world (resources, environment, economy, institutions, etc.) but very little to man's internal world, to his goals, desires, heart, mind, soul, and sensorial links with the planet and the universe. This second facet of our efforts at total comprehension must now receive urgent attention. As was the case for the environment, a public hearing must be given to those who have been dealing with these all-important subjects in the silence of their studies. This will be our royal avenue to a new under-standing of life, to full consciousness, and to the flowering of a happy, human society. It will also be the key to a peaceful world.

Pending that time, we must remember that life is all we have. If we leave it empty, it will remain empty. If we fill it with all our being, heart, mind, and soul, it will be full of all the marvels of heaven and earth.

As for myself, when the moment will come to close my eyes on this beautiful planet, my heart will thank and honor all those who gave me life and the warmth of love, and Him who permitted me to devote my earthly sojourn to peace, justice, and the betterment of the human condition in one of the noblest organizations ever born from the heart of man. I will go in peace and joy, thankful for having been blessed with the miracle of life.

I will have loved my life with passion, embraced it with fervor, cherished every single moment of it. I will have contemplated with wonder the sky and its running clouds, my brethren the humans, my sisters the flowers and the stars. I will have feasted unceasingly on the treasure of life in all its forms. I will not have dwelled in mediocre ambitions, vain hatred, and useless complaints.

I will depart with the belief that there is no end to the flow of life in the universe, that there is no death but only an unceasing change of worlds.

My conclusion would therefore be:

> decide to be happy
> render others happy
> proclaim your joy
> love passionately your miraculous life
> do not listen to promises
> do not wait for a better world
> be grateful for every moment of life
> switch on and keep on the positive buttons in yourself,
> those marked optimism, serenity, confidence,
> positive thinking, love
> pray and thank God every day
> meditate
> smile
> laugh
> whistle
> sing
> dance
> look with fascination at everything
> fill your lungs and heart with liberty
> be yourself fully and immensely
> act like a king unto Death
> feel God in your body, mind, heart, and soul
> and be convinced of eternal life and resurrection

* * * *

To order additional copies of this book, please contact:

Telephone: 800-727-2782

Email: Becky@ParaPublishing.com

Fax: 805-968-1379

Mail: Amare Media c/o Para Publishing
PO Box 8206
Santa Barbara, CA 93118-8206

Please make checks payable to **Amare Media LLC.** Each copy $12.95, plus $3.99 for shipping and handling. For all orders shipped to California, please add $1.00 (7.75% Sales Tax)

AMARE MEDIA LLC
PO Box 35360
Los Angeles, CA 90035-0360
www.amaremedia.com